The Welsh One Hundred

Walks to the 100 highest summits in Wales

First impression: April 1999
© Copyright Dafydd Andrews and Y Lolfa Cyf., 1999

Translated from the original Welsh version *Cant Cymru*
by the same author
Photographs: Jane Trudgill and the author

ISBN: 0 86243 497 1

Printed, published and bound in Wales by
Y Lolfa Cyf., Talybont, Ceredigion SY24 5AP
e-mail ylolfa@ylolfa.com
website www.ylolfa.com
phone +44 (0)1970 832 304
fax 832 782
isdn 832 813

The Welsh
One Hundred

DAFYDD ANDREWS

*This book is dedicated to my
mother and father*

Contents

	Introduction	7
1	The Carneddau	15
2	The Glyderau	27
3	Snowdon	37
4	Nantlle and Beddgelert	49
5	Blaenau Ffestiniog	57
6	Arenig	65
7	Berwyn	73
8	Aran	79
9	Rhinog	87
10	Cadair Idris	91
11	Pumlumon	97
12	The Black Mountain	101
13	Brecon Beacons	107
14	Carmarthen Fan	113
	The Welsh One Hundred	117

WARNING

Anyone who ventures into the mountains of Wales should know how to read a map and how to use a compass. This book is intended for use *with* a map and not for use *instead* of one. The book describes routes to the summits of the mountains of Wales in favourable conditions – that is to say, when it is clear enough for you to see the way ahead and when the mountains are not covered in snow or ice. Care should always be taken in the mountains. During the winter the high mountains of Wales are a place for experienced walkers and climbers.

Introduction

WALES is one of the most beautiful countries in the world and its hills and mountains are among its most obvious features. These mountains attract many walkers at all times of the year. If you visit Snowdonia at any weekend, particularly during the summer months, you will usually find the car parks full. The interest in mountain walking in Wales is not restricted to Snowdonia by any means, of course, though people naturally head there to see the country's rockiest and most striking mountains – and its highest too.

Even within Snowdonia National Park some mountains are more popular than others. As you might expect, Snowdon attracts more walkers and visitors than any other mountain in Wales. It is, after all, the highest mountain in Wales and it is also considerably higher than any mountain in England. No matter how many times you climb Snowdon – by day or by night, in summer or in winter – it is almost certain that there will be others there besides you. The same is true of Tryfan, the superb, impressive mountain which greets visitors as they travel westwards along the A5 from the direction of Capel Curig. Tryfan is the lowest of the peaks in Wales which is over 3000 feet – a figure which has some significance amongst mountaineers in Britain – but its outline and its rocky character immediately attract the eye. As with Snowdon, the summit of Tryfan is a place you will almost certainly never have to yourself.

Walkers tend to be attracted to a handful of popular mountains in Snowdonia, such as Snowdon and Tryfan, which leaves some of the other peaks in the National Park relatively quiet. This naturally has implications for erosion too, and one of the aims of this book is to attract walkers to other summits in our country, and not just the summits of Snowdonia. The Welsh One Hundred are spread all over the country and visiting them all will give you the chance to get to know many parts of Wales.

Anyone familiar with mountaineering in Britain is likely to have heard of the 'Munros'. These are, broadly speaking, the mountains of Scotland which are over 3000 feet in height and which were first listed by Sir Hugh Munro in 1891. Over the years, his original list has been revised on a number of occasions. The most recent revision was done in 1997 and there are now 284 Munros on the Scottish Mountaineering Club's official list. Several books listing these mountains are available (though many still contain the 277 peaks which were on the official list before the 1997 revision) and the challenge of reaching all their summits has caused an explosion of interest among walkers in Britain. But even for those who actually live in Scotland, completing all the Munros in a lifetime is a considerable feat which involves a great deal of travelling. For people living outside Scotland the challenge obviously involves even more travelling. Another aim of this book, therefore, is to create a mountaineering challenge here in Wales which for many people will involve less travelling, which (like the Munro challenge) is likely to be a long-term project and which includes all the highest mountains in the country – The Welsh One Hundred.

There has been much heated debate about how best to define a 'mountain' and about which peaks should be listed among the Munros of Scotland, and one is bound to say that over the years some odd decisions have been made. During the 1997 revision, many fundamental issues were raised yet again. In the final analysis, these matters involve a considerable amount of subjective appraisal and in preparing this book I have been keen to avoid the kind of controversy which has raged – and which continues to rage – in certain circles in Scotland. In point of fact, most of the mountains listed in the Welsh One Hundred select themselves and no-one would doubt that they deserve a place in the list. However, towards the lower end of the list especially, there are mountains which are not particularly impressive and some will no doubt argue that lower, more challenging peaks could have been included. Be that as it may, I followed the general principle that the list should include the *highest* mountains in Wales.

You have only to compare the mountains listed in two useful books about the mountains of Wales – *The Summits of Snowdonia* by Terry Marsh and *The Mountains of England and Wales, Volume 1: Wales* by

Tryfan

John and Anne Nuttall – and you will see straight away that there is no consensus about the mountains of Wales either. Both books illustrate the dangers involved in defining 'mountain' according to some mathematical formula, though one has to say that there is a good deal more common sense in Terry Marsh's book than in that of the Nuttalls. The mathematical method has given rise to other listings of Welsh mountains – some will have heard of the 'Marilyns' and the 'Hewitts', for example – but the great disadvantage of this approach is that it ignores factors which cannot be measured: the shape of the mountain, its appeal to the eye, the feeling it inspires, local perceptions and knowledge, the meanings of mountain names and so forth. Should Garnedd Uchaf be considered a separate mountain? Are there 14 or 15 mountains over 3000 feet in Wales? In the final analysis, these questions and many others cannot be settled with a tape measure.

At first glance, the book by the Nuttalls appears detailed and thorough, and indeed one has to admire their research into the history of different parts of Wales. But one soon gets the feeling that here are two people who, though they have walked all the mountains, are not really familiar with *Wales*. A fuller consideration of factors such as the names of the mountains, the opinions of local people and the way mountain walkers in Wales 'see' the mountains would surely have produced a different list and one which was not – in places – so down-right silly! Do the people of Llanberis really consider Llechog to be a separate mountain from Snowdon? Do the walkers of Wales think they are going up *two* mountains when they reach the top of Y Lliwedd and that Lliwedd Bach is a third, separate peak? You will hear people speak of going up 'y ddwy Aran' ('the two Arans') but in the view of the Nuttalls there are three mountains here. The rounded hill of Cadair Bronwen is made into two mountains and the barely perceptible hillocks of Ysgafell Wen into *three*! All this arises because they have settled on an arbitrary definition and stuck to it blindly. In the Spring 1997 edition of *Rambling Today* – the Ramblers'

Association magazine – the Nuttalls admit to a mistake in their book in the case of Cnicht, the so-called Matterhorn of Wales, which they now concede is actually *two* peaks and not one!

In selecting the Welsh One Hundred, I decided from the outset to avoid a narrow, mathematical definition of a peak and to base the list on a wider set of criteria. I accept that my method, too, is arbitrary – as any method is bound to be – but it will not send you off to visit an insignificant spot on the ground just because there happens to be a 50 foot drop in height all around. The Welsh One Hundred includes the mountains in Wales which walkers naturally and spontaneously seek to climb, which they instinctively feel to be mountains and/or which form part of an obvious mountaineering route.

Choosing the Routes

As explained earlier, this book aims to introduce walkers to the highest mountains in Wales. An attempt has been made to vary the routes in length. The book contains some walks which visit one mountain only whilst others involve visiting several mountains. However, many of the separate routes involving adjacent mountains can be joined together as they overlap. Similarly, some of the longer routes can be divided into two or three walks, and the route description contains suggestions which cover this. Even the purists who wish to ascend each of the Welsh One Hundred separately, from valley floor to summit, should be able to do so.

In general, the route chosen to each summit is the easiest or the most obvious. No doubt some walkers would prefer a more ambitious or challenging route in some cases – the north face and ridge of Tryfan for example – but the book aims to make these mountains accessible to a wide range of walkers. More testing routes can be tried later, when you re-visit familiar peaks and get to see them from a new perspective – which is surely one of the chief joys of the mountains.

Finally, it should be borne in mind also that the route descriptions given here are not intended to be used alone, and that either the 1:50 000 or 1:25 000 (or both) Ordnance Survey maps referred to at the beginning of each route should be used in conjunction with them. Everyone who walks the mountains of Wales should know how to read a map and how to use a compass.

How to use this book

THE MOUNTAINS OF WALES have been divided into fourteen groups and each group is discussed in a section of its own. The sections have been arranged in sequence from north to south (and from east to west when they are on the same 'level'). At the beginning of each section there is a brief general description of the mountains in the group.

Within each section there are individual walks which may contain one or more of the Welsh One Hundred. For each walk, information is provided under the following headings:

Mountain – this gives the name(s) of the mountain(s), the height of the mountain(s) in feet and in metres, and (in brackets) the position of the mountain(s) in the height list of the Welsh One Hundred which appears in the back of the book (along with a separate list of the peaks in alphabetical order for use as a page index).

Map – this gives the numbers of the relevant 1:50 000 and 1:25 000 scale maps and a grid reference (GR) for the summit of each mountain. The following abbreviations are used:
OS = Ordnance Survey Landranger map, the 1:50 000 scale maps with a red cover;
OL = Ordnance Survey Outdoor Leisure map, the 1:25 000 scale maps with a yellow cover;
P = Ordnance Survey Pathfinder map, the 1:25 000 scale maps with a green cover which are used when there is no OL map available for the area in question.

Translation – this gives a translation of the Welsh names of the mountains. See also the 'Translation and Pronunciation' section below.

Pronunciation – this provides a guide on the pronunciation of the names of the mountains for people not familiar with the orthography of Welsh. See also the 'Translation and Pronunciation' section below.

Starting Point – including a grid reference and information about parking cars.

Distance and **Ascent** – this provides an estimate of the length of the walk described and of how much ascent is involved. It should be borne in mind that the ascent figure will affect how long the walk will take.

Estimated Time – as everyone's pace is different, this figure is for comparison only. After walking a few of the routes, however, walkers will gain an idea as to how to adapt the figure to their own pace.

Route – This provides the walker with a brief description of the route and is not intended as a step by step account of the way to the summit. Reference is made to features which are clearly marked on the 1:50 000 maps and no names are used which do not appear on these maps. Occasionally, however, a name found on the more detailed 1:25 000 maps is added in brackets where it could be of some help.

It should be borne in mind that the fact that a route appears in this book does not automatically mean that a right of way exists. The great majority of these walks, however, are on public footpaths or in places where the right to roam is an established tradition. Reference is made in the text to any known instances of conflict on access issues. Personally, I have never experienced any difficulties on the routes described here. Circumstances can change suddenly, however, and I would be interested and grateful to hear of any difficulties experienced by users of this book.

Translation and Pronunciation

Translation

Only a rash person would claim to know for certain the meanings of all the names of the mountains in Wales, even though Welsh mountain names – like the Welsh names of towns and villages – are generally easier to understand than many in England. A Welsh speaker will have no difficulty in telling you what a name like Mynydd Mawr or Y Foel Goch means, whereas the meanings of names like Skiddaw, Helvellyn and Blencathra in the Lake District, for example, are not immediately intelligible to English speakers.

Having said that, several Welsh mountain names can be problematic too. A good example is Y Lliwedd in the Snowdon group. On the face of it, we have the word 'lliw' = 'colour' or 'hue'. Simple. But the word is possibly cognate with a Breton word meaning 'a troop of soldiers'. Not likely as an interpretation, you might think. But this is an area with many mythical associations. Rhita the Giant is supposedly buried on the top of Snowdon, King Arthur's men are said to be resting in a nearby cave and the names of neighbouring features such as Bwlch y Saethau (The Pass of the Arrows) suggest that the interpretation is not necessarily ridiculous. In brief, it always pays to be cautious when translating old names.

Pronunciation

Attempting to say correctly the name of the mountain you are to climb is part of the process of getting to know it, and part of the fun of being in a different mountain environment. The pronunciation of Welsh names can be difficult for non-Welsh speakers but this need not be so. Welsh orthography is perfectly straightforward. Problems arise because Welsh has certain sounds which do not occur in English – such as the 'ch' sound and the ubiquitous 'll' – and because familiar sounds occur in unfamiliar places.

To help, I have tried to write the names of the mountains as if they were being spelt in English. I have used italics to identify the syllables where the stress lies (in Welsh, the stress is normally on the last syllable but one). The system is far from perfect but it will give you a pronunciation which is at least reasonably close to being accurate. Listen to the locals if you get a chance and bear in mind that there will be minor variations in pronunciation from area to area, just as no Geordie speaks like a Liverpudlian or a Londoner.

The following will help:-
ll – position your tongue as if you were about to say 'l' and blow out hard (rather like the 'tl' sound in the middle of the word 'antler').
r – the letter is always rolled, and occurs at the front of the mouth (like the Scots and unlike the French).
ch – as in 'loch'.
dd – I always represent this with the letters 'th', but it is invariably the soft sounding 'th' as in 'this' and not the hard sounding 'th' as in 'think'.

Despite the great temptation to change the spellings of the names of some of the mountains seen on the Ordnance Survey maps so that they are consistent with modern Welsh orthography and with the syntax of Welsh, I have not done so unless there was an obvious blunder. Even if this appears linguistically indefensible to some, it does at least have the advantage of consistency with other books about the mountains of Wales.

In keeping with developing practice, I have not translated the terms for features such as 'Afon' (river), 'Nant' (stream) and 'Bwlch' (pass) where they are clearly a part of a name and appear as such on Ordnance Survey maps. I also use the word 'llyn' (lake) standing alone in the text, just as 'loch' is used in Scotland.

I would like to take this opportunity to thank the Lolfa Press for their usual assistance and support and also a number of other people to whom I am indebted for their help and company during the preparation of the original Welsh version of this book and also during the process of preparing this translation. I would particularly like to mention my wife Jane, her parents Peter and Juliet Trudgill, and Menna Hughes who gave me practical assistance and made several useful suggestions. Thanks also to a number of friends and relatives who have shown an interest in the book.

Finally, I would like to dedicate this English version to my father and mother. Now each has a version in his/her own language!

1. The Carneddau

BETWEEN LLYN OGWEN to the south and the sea to the north, between Bethesda to the west and the Conwy valley to the east, there lies a large group of mountains which is now known by the name 'The Carneddau'. A number of Wales' highest mountains are to be found in this splendid group. Among them are Carnedd Llewelyn and Carnedd Dafydd, named after two of Wales' most famous princes, and the first element in their name has long been used as the name for this entire group of mountains. In general, the southern mountains of the group are rocky — though there are grassy slopes to be found here as well. You will find large lakes, dramatic cliffs and rock faces, as well as a long, high-level ridge which offers spectacular views in all directions. The northern hills in this group are more grassy and are generally easier under foot. They are also less frequented.

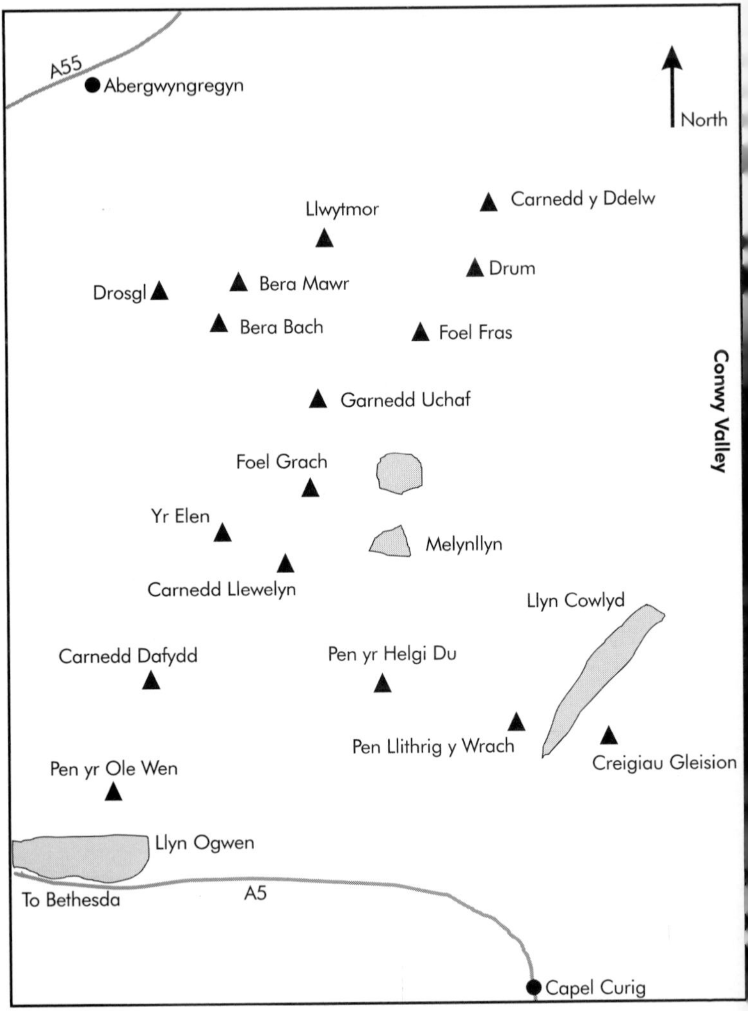

A55

● Abergwyngregyn

North

▲ Carnedd y Ddelw

Llwytmor
▲

▲ Drum

Drosgl ▲

▲ Bera Mawr

▲ Foel Fras

▲ Bera Bach

Conwy Valley

▲ Garnedd Uchaf

Foel Grach
▲

Yr Elen
▲

Melynllyn

▲ Carnedd Llewelyn

Llyn Cowlyd

Carnedd Dafydd
▲

Pen yr Helgi Du
▲

Pen yr Ole Wen
▲

Pen Llithrig y Wrach ▲

▲ Creigiau Gleision

Llyn Ogwen

To Bethesda   A5

● Capel Curig

Map: OS 115, OL 17: GR 689692

Translation: Big Grey Hill

Pronunciation: *Lloo*-itmore

Starting Point: Bont Newydd, a little to the south east of Abergwyngregyn, GR 663720. There is space for quite a number of cars.

Distance: 6 miles / 9.6 kilometres. **Ascent:** 2526 ft / 770 metres

Estimated Time: 3-5 hours

Route: Go through the gate by the bridge and follow the river to a footbridge. Cross the footbridge and turn right along the wide path which leads to the Rhaeadr-fawr waterfall. Soon after you have passed below the electricity cables – shortly before reaching the cottage called Nant (GR 666713) which has an information room in an outbuilding – you will see a narrower, signposted path leading off left into the forest. Go through the wood along this path and, when you finally emerge from it, cross the scree and continue over the rocks towards Rhaeadr-fawr. Follow the Afon Goch to a sheepfold and from there head east up steep, rough slopes in the direction of the flat shoulder below the summit of Llwytmor. Then head south-east to reach the summit. The small cairn is the highest point. From the summit drop south to the col below, to avoid rocks, and turn west-south-west crossing rough ground to pick up a path above the Afon Goch.

Mountain: Bera Mawr, 2605 ft / 794 m (38); Bera Bach, 2648 ft / 807 m (33); Drosgl, 2487 ft / 758 m (49)

Map: OS 115, OL 17: GR 675683, GR 672677, GR 664680
Translation: Large Hayrick, Little Hayrick, Rough Hill
Pronunciation: Beara *Ma*-oor, Beara Baach, *Dross*-gull
Starting Point: Bont Newydd, a little to the south-east of Abergwyngregyn, GR 663720. There is space for quite a number of cars.
Distance: 7 miles / 11.2 kilometres. **Ascent:** 2493 ft / 760 metres
Estimated Time: 3-6 hours

Route: Go through the gate by the bridge and follow the river to a footbridge. Cross the footbridge and turn right along the wide path which leads to the Rhaeadr-fawr waterfall. Soon after you pass below the electricity cables – shortly before reaching the cottage called Nant (GR 666713) which has an information room in an outbuilding – you will see another, narrower path leading off left into the forest. Go through the wood along this path and when you emerge from it cross the scree and continue over the rocks above Rhaeadr-fawr. Follow the Afon Goch for about one hundred metres until the land starts to level out. Cross the river and climb south-west up the slopes of Bera Mawr. The striking rocky summit of Bera Mawr comes into view in the south-east as you reach the flat ridge and a faint path leads towards it. The summit rock can be climbed easily on its northern side. From here, the rocks of Bera Bach can be seen to the south. Aim for the left (east) side of these rocks. From the summit of Bera Bach a clear path leads to Drosgl in the west. From Drosgl's stony summit, follow the mountain's northern ridge back to the Nature Reserve keeping between the Afon Gam and the Afon Rhaeadr-bach. Cross the fence at a stile and turn right. At the foot of Rhaeadr-fawr, cross the river and return to Bont Newydd along the path northwards.

Mountain: Foel Grach, 3202 ft / 976 m (8); Garnedd Uchaf, 3038 ft / 926 m (12); Foel Fras, 3091 ft / 942 m (11); Drum, 2526 ft / 770 m (45); Carnedd y Ddelw, 2257 ft / 688 m (82)

Map: OS 115, OL 17: GR 689659, GR 687669, GR 696682, GR 708696, GR 708705

Translation: Scabby Hill, Highest Cairn, Rough Hill, Ridge, Cairn of the Idol

Pronunciation: Voil Graach, *Garn*-eth *Ich*-av, Voil Vraas, Drim, *Carn*-eth uh *Thel*-oo

Starting Point: Cwm Eigiau – three miles south-west of Tal-y-bont in the Conwy Valley, GR 732663. There is a car park where the minor road comes to an end.

Distance: 11 miles / 17.6 kilometres. **Ascent:** 2743 ft / 836 metres

Estimated Time: 4-8 hours

Route: Cross the stile and follow the track which leads to Melynllyn. Either take to the ridge on your left from the highest point of the track or proceed to a ruined mill and cross rough ground westwards to the llyn's southern shore. From there, climb south-west up steep slopes avoiding the rocks of Craig Fawr on their left (south). Once on the ridge, turn north-west and head for the summit of Foel Grach. There is a mountain refuge hut immediately below the summit. A gentle stroll northwards brings you to the summit of Garnedd Uchaf. Continue north-east from there to reach the wall which crosses the boulder-strewn summit of Foel-fras, the northernmost of Wales' 3000 ft peaks. You can return to the car park from here by descending south-east and following the Afon Garreg Wen to the path which leads to the ruin of Maeneira (GR 727673). However, if you want to complete the whole walk today, an excellent path leads over short grass to Drum in the north-east and onwards to Garnedd y Ddelw. From there, return to the top of Drum and turn south-east to reach a broad, level spur. From the end of the spur, turn south down steep slopes and then rough, grassy ground to reach the Afon Ddu. Either cross it here or lower down by a stile and follow it – with the fence to your left – to where it joins the Afon Dulyn where you pick up a path which leads to Maeneira and which continues south to rejoin the track to the car park.

Mountain: Carnedd Llewelyn, 3491 ft / 1064 m (3)

Map: OS 115, OL 17: GR 684644
Translation: Llewelyn's Cairn
Pronunciation: *Carn*-eth Llew-*el*-in
Starting Point: The A5 – opposite the Glan Dena plantation, slightly to the east of Llyn Ogwen, GR 668605. There is ample room to park on the southern side of the road.
Distance: 6 miles / 9.6 kilometres. **Ascent:** 2487 ft / 758 metres
Estimated Time: 3-6 hours

Route: Take the road through the plantation at Glan Dena. Just before reaching the farm of Tal y Llyn Ogwen, a signpost directs you to the right. Follow the stone wall to a stile and cross it. Follow the Afon Lloer, first on the eastern side and then the western side, for about half a mile (0.8 kilometres) over steep slopes and cross a second stile below the eastern ridge of Pen yr Ole Wen. Where the river bends before Ffynnon Lloer, the path begins to level out and hugs the river (GR 666619). Cross the river here and walk north over grassy slopes (Rhos Bodesi) keeping to the east of the stony slopes below the summit of Carnedd Dafydd. Having reached the ridge of Cefn Ysgolion Duon with its stunning views, turn right and follow the path towards Carnedd Llewelyn. The rocky sections of this path can be avoided by descending a little on the right. The summit of Carnedd Llewelyn is an enormous stony plateau and there is a stone shelter on the highest point.

Map: OS 115, OL 17: GR 674651
Translation: Hill of the Deer
Pronunciation: Uhr *El*-en
Starting Point: Road junction in Gerlan, Bethesda GR 634663.
One or two cars can be parked near this junction. **The two rivers mentioned in this walk can be difficult to cross in spate.**
Distance: 6 miles / 9.6 kilometres. **Ascent:** 2461 ft / 750 metres
Estimated Time: 3-7 hours

Route: From the junction take the minor road to the north-east. There are several bends in the road, which changes into a mere stone track once the houses are left behind, but after about half a mile (0.8 kilometres) you reach the track below the slopes of Gyrn Wigau which takes you north-east once more. Follow this track for about another half a mile (0.8 kilometres) and then – before reaching an old quarry – turn south-east, following the wall downhill. Cross the Afon Caseg and turn south-south-east, aiming for the western ridge of Yr Elen (Braich y Brisgyll) and the 512 metre height spot on the 1:50 000 map. Follow the grassy ridge south-east for a little over a mile (1.6 kilometres), cross Foel Ganol and continue towards the steep rocky slope leading to the summit of Yr Elen. The cairn above the east ridge is the summit. To vary the route back, you could return to the 512 height spot and turn south over wet ground, cross the Afon Llafar and go up to the nearby path which leads back to Gerlan.

Mountain: Carnedd Dafydd, 3412 ft / 1044 m (4)

Map: OS 115, OL 17: GR 663630
Translation: Dafydd's Cairn
Pronunciation: *Carn*-eth *Dav*-ith
Starting Point: The A5 – opposite the Glan Dena plantation,
slightly to the east of Llyn Ogwen, GR 668605. There is ample room
to park on the southern side of the road.
Distance: 4-5 miles / 6.4-8 kilometres. **Ascent:** 2408 ft / 734
metres
Estimated Time: 2-4 hours

Route: Take the road through the plantation at Glan Dena. Just before
reaching the farm of Tal y Llyn Ogwen, a signpost directs you to the
right. Follow the stone wall to a stile and cross it. Follow the Afon
Lloer, first on the eastern side and then the western side, for about half
a mile (0.8 kilometres) over steep slopes and cross a second stile below
the eastern ridge of Pen yr Ole Wen. Where the river bends before
Ffynnon Lloer, the path begins to level out and hugs the river (GR
666619). Cross the river here and walk north over grassy slopes (Rhos
Bodesi) keeping to the east of the stony slopes below the summit of
Carnedd Dafydd. As you reach the ridge of Cefn Ysgolion Duon the
view changes dramatically and Cwmglas Mawr, the cliffs of Ysgolion
Duon, Carnedd Llewelyn and much more comes into view. Turn west
and follow the edge of the cliff before turning to reach the stony summit
of Carnedd Dafydd. Rather than returning the way you came, you could
follow the path to the south-west around Cwm Lloer, climb to the
summit of Pen-yr-Ole-Wen and follow its east ridge back to the bend
in the Afon Lloer.

Map: OS 115, OL 17: GR 656619
Translation: Peak of the White Slope
Pronunciation: Pen-uhr-ol-eh-*when*
Starting Point: The A5 – opposite the Glan Dena plantation, slightly to the east of Llyn Ogwen, GR 668605. There is ample room to park on the southern side of the road.
Distance: 3½ miles / 5.6 kilometres. **Ascent:** 2192 ft / 668 metres
Estimated Time: 2-4 hours

Route: Take the road through the plantation at Glan Dena. Just before reaching the farm of Tal y Llyn Ogwen, a signpost directs you to the right. Follow the stone wall to a stile and cross it. Follow the Afon Lloer, first on the eastern side and then the western side, for about half a mile (0.8 kilometres) over steep slopes and cross a second stile below the eastern ridge of Pen yr Ole Wen. Where the river bends before Ffynnon Lloer, the path begins to level out and hugs the river (GR 666619). Here, climb the rise on your left and cross the flat ground towards the ridge. At first there is no clear path but things improve. High on the mountain, minor paths here and there allow you glimpses of the cliffs on the north side of Pen yr Ole Wen and Cwm Lloer far below. Take care not to be drawn onto this north face of the mountain, however. Remain on the ridge and a steep final pull brings you to the flat, stony summit. The stone cairn – and not the triangulation point – marks the summit.

Map: OS 115, OL 17: GR 698630, GR 716623

Translation: The Peak (or Head) of the Black Hound, The Slippery Peak (or Head) of the Witch

Pronunciation: Pen-uhr-hell-ghee-*dee*, Pen *Llith*-rig uh Oor-*aach*

Starting Point: Gwern Gof Isaf farm on the A5, about 3 miles (4.8 kilometres) north-west of the village of Capel Curig, GR 685603. There is a charge for parking.

Distance: 7 miles / 11.2 kilometres. **Ascent:** 2461 ft / 750 metres

Estimated Time: 3-6 hours

Route: From the car park, rather than walk along the busy A5, walk past the farmhouse of Gwern Gof Isaf and turn along the old Holyhead road in the direction of Helyg, GR 691602, where you can cross the main road and take another road which leads to the farms at Tal-y-braich. After about 300m, you have to leave this road and follow a path which could easily be missed. Having set off along the road, you will see a building below you on the right beside the A5. It belongs to a mountaineering club and has a private car park. Once you have passed behind this building, the road crosses a stream and you see a small, level area on the left where farm vehicles turn. Immediately beyond this level area (GR 694603) a faint path can be seen heading north-east over rough ground towards a stile over a stone wall in the distance. Once over the stile, keep to the same direction until you reach a bridge over the leat which carries water to Llyn Cowlyd in the east. Cross the bridge and follow Pen yr Helgi Du's long ridge (called Y Braich) northwards until you reach the summit which is marked by a cairn. From the summit, turn south-east at first and head down to Bwlch y Tri Marchog. Climb the steep slopes of Pen Llithrig y Wrach. From the summit of Pen Llithrig y Wrach go south, following the edge of the cliff until you reach a bridge on the col (Bwlch Cowlyd) where the leat releases its water into Llyn Cowlyd. Now turn west and follow a good path which turns south in about three quarters of a mile (1.2 kilometres) before crossing the Afon Bedol to the farmhouse of Tal-y-braich-isaf. From there, take the path to the farm of Tal-y-braich-uchaf in the west where you reach the road back to the A5.

Pen yr Helgi Du and Pen Llithrig y Wrach

Pen Llithrig y Wrach and Creigiau Gleision

Mountain: Creigiau Gleision, 2224 ft / 678 m (89)

Map: OS 115, OL 17: GR 729615

Translation: Grey Rocks

Pronunciation: *Craig*-ee-I *Glace*-eeon

Starting Point: Capel Curig, GR 720582. Car park on the old Holyhead road. There is a charge for parking.

Distance: 8 miles / 12.8 kilometres. **Ascent:** 2054 ft / 626 metres

Estimated Time: 3-6 hours

Route: From the car park, go back to the A5 and cross it. Opposite the junction, a little to the left of the church, a footpath climbs gently over a field and then heads east. Ignore minor paths which lead to the nearby rocks where climbers come to practise. The path drops gently down through trees and then emerges to pass the striking rocky outcrop of Clogwyn-mawr on the left. Having crossed a stream (Nant y Geuallt, GR 732582) the path splits into two. Take the path to the left (north-east) which leads into a wide valley and climbs very slowly to the col above Llyn Crafnant. On the col, this path also splits into two. Take the left path. Almost immediately, you have to leave it and head towards another path which climbs steeply up a slope to the summit of Crimpiau in the south-east. From this summit, Creigiau Gleision can be seen to the north beyond Craig Wen and another top. The path heads for the western side of Craig Wen. A detour can be made to the summit of Craig Wen by leaving the main path and following another path or by scrambling directly over the rocks, rejoining the main path below the north side of Craig Wen. Here it crosses a wet col (Bwlch Mignog) and continues over grassy slopes towards Creigiau Gleision. Immediately below the summit there is a flat area. From here, go up through the rocks to reach the summit cairn. The return journey can be varied by heading for the col above the southern end of Llyn Cowlyd (Bwlch Cowlyd) to the south-west. First, go back to the flat area below the summit of Creigiau Gleision. Then, head directly for Bwlch Cowlyd down slopes covered in heather and thick grass (Llethr Gwyn). From Bwlch Cowlyd, where a leat discharges its water into Llyn Cowlyd below, there is a good path which goes down to the A5 in the south passing behind Tal-y-Waun farm. Having reached the A5 turn left to return to Capel Curig.

2. The Glyderau

THIS GROUP OF MOUNTAINS lies between Llyn Ogwen and Llanberis. As with the Carneddau, the group derives its name from two of its main peaks, Glyder Fach and Glyder Fawr. Some of the most striking and memorable mountains in the whole of Wales are to be found here. The first sighting of Tryfan as you travel westwards along the A5 is an exciting and impressive experience, even for many people who would never set foot on a mountain. Its splendid rocky north face seems to rise directly from the waters of Llyn Ogwen and offers a real mountaineering challenge. As one approaches Llyn Ogwen the graceful curves of Y Garn, its ridges reaching out towards you, come into view beyond the far end of the lake. The summits of Glyder Fach and Glyder Fawr are hidden, but the northern flanks of these twin mountains appear as a wall of rock when you stand at the lake shore. These are rocky mountains with fine ridges — excellent terrain for scrambling and climbing. Elidir Fawr and, in particular, the mountains of Nant Ffrancon offer gentler, grass-covered slopes where you can stretch your legs once more.

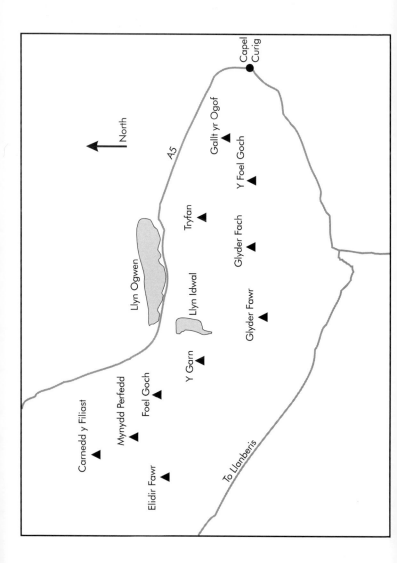

28

Map: OS 115, OL 17: GR 664594
Translation: Pointed Peak
Pronunciation: *Truh*-van
Starting Point: The A5 – Idwal Cottage Youth Hostel at the western end of Llyn Ogwen, GR 650603. Large car park. Fee payable.
Distance: 3 miles / 5 kilometres. **Ascent:** 2007 ft / 612 metres
Estimated Time: 2-4 hours

Route: From the car park take the stone path, which has been laid to prevent further erosion, south-east towards Tryfan. Where this path turns sharply to the right (south-west) towards Llyn Idwal, carry straight on over grassy, stony ground and climb to Llyn Bochlwyd on another pitched path. Cross Nant Bochlwyd – the stream which flows from the llyn towards the A5 – and follow the clear path above the llyn to the south-south-east. Once past the end of the llyn, the path turns south-east once more and starts to climb a rocky slope to the col (Bwlch Tryfan) where there is a stone wall. From here turn northwards (left). You will see the high rocky outcrop of Tryfan's Far South Peak ahead of you. Trend left to avoid it and scramble over the rocks and boulders to the summit of Tryfan itself. The two monoliths on the summit – known as Adam and Eve – are a feature which is unique in the mountains of Britain.

Mountain: Glyder Fach, 3261 ft / 994 m (6)

Map: OS 115, OL 17: GR 656583
Translation: Lesser Heap
Pronunciation: *Glud*-air Vaach
Starting Point: The A5 – Idwal Cottage Youth Hostel at the western end of Llyn Ogwen, GR 650603. Large car park. Fee payable.
Distance: 3½ miles / 5.6 kilometres. **Ascent:** 2267 ft / 691 metres
Estimated Time: 2-4 hours

Route: From the car park take the stone path south-east, which has been laid to prevent further erosion. Where this path turns sharply to the right (south-west) towards Llyn Idwal, carry straight on over grassy, stony ground and climb to Llyn Bochlwyd on another pitched path. Cross Nant Bochlwyd – the stream which flows from the llyn towards the A5 – and follow the clear path above the llyn to the south-south-east. Once past the end of the lake, the path turns south-east once more and starts to climb a rocky slope to the col (Bwlch Tryfan) where there is a stone wall. Cross one of the stiles and turn right (south-west). By following the wall you would reach the rocky ridge known as Bristley Ridge which makes a splendid scrambling route to the summit of the mountain. For walkers, it is easier to head left away from the ridge and climb the steep scree. The summit of Glyder Fach is a flat, stony expanse and the highest point is a large pile of enormous boulders. From the summit, carry straight on south-west and by-pass the huge, weird rock pile of Castell y Gwynt by descending to the left and going around it. Once across Bwlch y Ddwy Glyder, follow the cliff edge until you reach Y Gribin, the ridge which heads down northwards. The upper part of the ridge is rocky but much easier ground is soon reached. A clear path now heads out towards Llyn Bochlwyd. Either take this path or head on northwards over grassy slopes and then wet ground to pick up the path back to the car park.

Map: OS 115, OL 17: GR 642580
Translation: Greater Heap
Pronunciation: *Glud*-air *Va*-oor
Starting Point: The A5 – Idwal Cottage Youth Hostel at the western end of Llyn Ogwen, GR 650603. Large car park. Fee payable.
Distance: 4½ miles / 7.2 kilometres. **Ascent:** 2283 ft / 696 metres
Estimated Time: 3-5 hours

Route: From the car park take the stone path south-east as if heading for Tryfan. Soon the path turns sharply to the right (south-west) towards Llyn Idwal. At the llyn, cross the stile and follow its eastern shore. This clear path takes you past the Idwal slabs – where many come to climb – at the far end of the llyn before turning upwards in the direction of Twll Du (The Devil's Kitchen). Do not go into Twll Du itself. The path turns left below the rock face and then turns right and emerges from the stony ground into an obvious channel as the ground levels out. Immediately before reaching Llyn y Cŵn, turn left and take a path which climbs very steeply to the stony summit of Glyder Fawr. There are two large piles of rocks near each other on the summit which appear to be of the same height. The one on the right is actually higher. From the summit proceed east and follow the rim of the northern cwm (Cwm Cneifion) until you reach Y Gribin, the ridge which heads down northwards. The upper part of the ridge is rocky but much easier ground is soon reached. A clear path now heads out towards Llyn Bochlwyd. Either take this path or head on northwards over grassy slopes and then wet ground to pick up the path back to the car park.

Map: OS 115, OL 17: GR 631596

Translation: The Cairn

Pronunciation: Uh *Garn*

Starting Point: The A5 – Idwal Cottage Youth Hostel at the western end of Llyn Ogwen, GR 650603. Large car park. Fee payable.

Distance: 4½ miles / 7.2 kilometres. **Ascent:** 2113 ft / 644 metres

Estimated Time: 3-5 hours

Route: From the car park take the stone path south-east as if heading for Tryfan. Soon the path turns sharply to the right (south-west) towards Llyn Idwal. At the llyn, cross the stile and follow its northern shore before ascending over grassy slopes towards the striking north-east ridge of Y Garn. Follow the path along this ridge to the summit. From the shelter on the summit, head south-south-east down to Llyn y Cŵn. If time allows, it is worth detouring to see the chasm of Twll Du by following the stream which flows from the llyn. There is certainly no way down here for walkers though. Return to the llyn and follow the path  along its shore and head left just before reaching the rocky slopes of Glyder Fawr. A long, grassy channel leads you to a stony area where you should take care to head left for the rock face and not carry straight on ahead as there is a cliff which cannot be seen. Follow the stony path down to the foot of Twll Du and turn right when you reach the stream which rushes from it. As you descend through rocks, you will see that a clear path can be taken on either side of Llyn Idwal to return to its northern end.

Mountain: Elidir Fawr, 3018 ft / 920 m (14); Mynydd Perfedd, 2667 ft / 813 m (31); Carnedd y Filiast, 2697 ft / 822 m (30); Foel Goch 2726 ft / 831m (27)

Map: OS 115, OL 17: GR 612613, GR 623619, GR 620628, GR 629612

Translation: Great Cairn of Elidir, Middle Mountain, Cairn of the Greyhound Bitch, Red Hill

Pronunciation: El-*id*-eer *Va*-oor, *Mun*-eathe *Pair*-veth, *Carn*-eth uh *Vill*-yast

Starting Point: The village of Nant Peris, about 2 miles (3.2 kilometres) south-east of Llanberis, GR 606584. There is a large car park nearby.

Distance: 7-8 miles / 11.2-12.8 kilometres. **Ascent:** 3392 ft / 1034 metres

Estimated Time: 4-8 hours

Route: Leave the main road and take the lane by the chapel. At first the lane follows the Afon Gafr and then turns north and passes scattered houses as it climbs from the valley. Having passed through a gate, stay on the lane and when you reach the next wall you will see a sign directing you to the right towards a stile. From there the path continues to another stile where the open mountain is reached. The path now climbs to the Afon Dudodyn and follows its eastern bank. When you reach a bridge (GR 609595) cross it and climb the steep slope ahead. Walk north until you reach a stile in the uppermost wall of the field system. The path now heads diagonally up across steep grassy slopes to the summit of Elidir Fawr. From there, follow the mountain's narrow, eastern ridge past the end of Marchlyn Mawr Reservoir and climb north-east to the top of Mynydd Perfedd. Now head north until you reach the striking rock formation (known as the Atlantic Slabs) above the next cwm (Cwm Graianog) and follow the edge in the direction of Carnedd y Filiast. A small cairn shows the highest point. Return to Mynydd Perfedd and from its summit head south-south-east to reach the clear path from Elidir Fawr once more. Leave this path again as you approach Foel Goch and climb steeply south-east to reach the mountain's summit. To return to Nant Peris, descend west, crossing the Afon Dudodyn, and take the path back to the bridge or take the path on the eastern side of Afon Gafr.

Elidir Fawr and Y Garn

Tryfan

Map: OS 115, OL 17: GR 678582, GR 685586
Translation: The Red Hill, The Steep Slope of the Cave
Pronunciation: Uh Voil *Goch*, Gallt uhr *Og*-ov
Starting Point: Capel Curig, GR 720582. Car park on the old Holyhead road. There is a charge for parking.
Distance: 6-7 miles / 9.6-11.2 kilometres. **Ascent:** 2231 ft / 680 metres
Estimated Time: 3-6 hours

Route: Leave the car park and turn right, heading north along the old Holyhead road. This tarmac road comes to an end in front of a house on the left. Go through the gate ahead and turn immediately left, following the fence. Where the fence turns left to go behind the house, there are two tracks – one follows the fence and the other is slightly higher up. Follow this higher track which narrows to a path as it slowly climbs to the broad grassy ridge of Cefn y Capel, which is wet in places. In about a mile and a half (2.4 kilometres) the path starts climbing steeply up grassy slopes towards Gallt yr Ogof. However, rather than heading straight up Gallt yr Ogof, the path turns below its rocky upper slopes and heads for Y Foel Goch, whose summit can clearly be seen about half a mile away (0.8 kilometres). Go to the top of Y Foel Goch first. From the summit cairn, set off back the way you came but take another path which heads for the summit of Gallt yr Ogof passing a small llyn on the col between the two mountains. From the summit of Gallt yr Ogof follow the ridge north-east until a fence comes into sight below the rocks on the ridge itself. A clear path ahead tempts you onwards, but the aim now is to turn left (west) and descend carefully over rocky, heathery ground to the cwm below (Cwm Gwern Gof) and follow the stream (Nant yr Ogof) to the farm of Gwern Gof Isaf. (If you decide to follow the fence on the ridge, bear in mind that there is a high vertical cliff ahead which appears with virtually no warning where the fence ends, and you will notice that the path trends left onto a heathery slope to avoid it.) Having reached the stone wall near the farm, turn right and follow the old Holyhead road all the way back to Capel Curig.

3. Snowdon

AS EVERYONE KNOWS, Snowdon is the highest mountain in Wales and it is also higher than any mountain in England. Because of its height it is a very popular mountain, especially during the summer months, and many of the walkers seen on its various paths and ridges are often comparatively inexperienced in mountaineering terms. The presence of numerous walkers, combined with the summit cafe, the railway from Llanberis and the carefully constructed paths, create in some people the feeling that Snowdon is not worth climbing as regards views and that it is an 'easy' or safe mountain. These impressions are in many ways ill-founded. Each of the paths to the summit of Snowdon has its delights — even the near highway from Llanberis — and the view from the summit is splendid in all directions. Some claim even to have seen the mountains of Ireland on a particularly clear day. It should also be borne in mind that the summit of Snowdon — compared to the summits of many mountains in Snowdonia — is some considerable distance from the road. Furthermore, Snowdon sees many accidents every year, some fatal. In the vicinity of Snowdon is the famous Crib Goch (see cover photograph), whose narrow ridge makes it one of the most valued, exciting and popular mountaineering achievements in the British Isles — though in winter conditions it is a place for experienced walkers and climbers who have the right equipment and who know how to use it. To the north lies Moel Eilio, from whose summit you get a view almost unrivalled in the mountains of Britain.

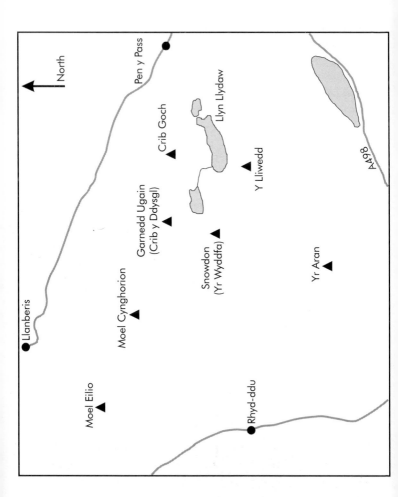

North

Pen y Pass

Crib Goch

Llyn Llydaw

Y Lliwedd

Garnedd Ugain
(Crib y Ddysgl)

Snowdon
(Yr Wyddfa)

Yr Aran

Llanberis

Moel Cynghorion

A498

Moel Eilio

Rhyd-ddu

Map: OS 115, OL 17: GR 610544
Translation: The Burial Mound (of Rhita the Giant)
Pronunciation: Uhr *With*-vaa
Starting Point: Pen y Pass car park at the top of Llanberis Pass, GR 647556. There is a charge for parking.
Distance: 6 miles / 9.6 kilometres. **Ascent:** 2382 ft / 726 metres
Estimated Time: 4-7 hours

Route: There are several routes to the summit of Snowdon and they should all be sampled as there are many interesting facets to the mountain. One obvious advantage of starting at the top of the Llanberis Pass is that it is higher than the other starting points. An approach from this direction also gives you the best view of the mountains in the Snowdon Horseshoe – Crib Goch, Garnedd Ugain, Snowdon itself and Y Lliwedd – in their magnificent rocky splendour. Take the wide stony path from the western end of the car park (behind the building) with Crib Goch – and not Snowdon, as many tend to think – ahead of you. This track, which is called the Pig or Pyg Track, climbs slowly up to a col (Bwlch Moch) where the view changes dramatically as the cliffs of Snowdon and Y Lliwedd come into view across Llyn Llydaw. Ignore the path which climbs towards Crib Goch. The path to Snowdon continues slightly downhill at first, following a fence. Above Glaslyn the Miners' Track climbs up to join this path (GR 614548) and soon you reach the stone paving which has been

put in place to avoid further erosion as the route zig-zags up to the col (Bwlch Glas) which is marked with a standing stone. Turn left and follow the railway to the summit. Return the way you came or take the Miners' Track, which also leads back to the car park.

Map: OS 115, OL 17: GR 624552
Translation: Red Ridge
Pronunciation: Creeb Goch
Starting Point: Pen y Pass car park at the top of Llanberis Pass, GR 647556. There is a charge for parking. **In winter conditions, Crib Goch is a serious mountaineering undertaking best left to equipped, experienced walkers and climbers.**
Distance: 4 miles / 6.4 kilometres. **Ascent:** 1844 ft / 562 metres
Estimated Time: 4-6 hours

Route: Take the wide stony path from the western end of the car park (behind the building) with Crib Goch ahead of you. This track, which is called the Pig or Pyg Track, climbs slowly up to a col (Bwlch Moch) where it divides into two. The upper path heads straight towards the impressive rock face of Crib Goch. At the face, you will certainly need to use your hands to negotiate a short section of what is an easy-grade climb. A scramble along the crest then gives the best views and eventually brings you up to the narrow level ridge for which the mountain is rightly famous. The exposure on both sides is considerable, particularly to the north, and on the narrowest sections it is best to stand a little below the ridge on the south side (left) and use the rock as a handrail. The highest point of the mountain can be seen to be about half way along the ridge. Rather than turn back, continue to the series of rock pinnacles at the end of the ridge. These can either be climbed directly or avoided by dropping to the south (left). Descend to the col between Crib Goch and Garnedd Ugain (Bwlch Coch). Crib Goch is usually climbed en route to Snowdon via Garnedd Ugain but from Bwlch Coch a fence can be followed downwards to the path which leads from Snowdon back to Bwlch Moch and onwards to the car park.

Crib Goch ▶

Mountain: Garnedd Ugain (sometimes called Crib y Ddysgl), 3494 ft / 1065 m (2)

Map: OS 115, OL 17: GR 611552
Translation: Higin's Cairn (Ridge of the Dish)
Pronunciation: *Garn*-eth *Igg*-ine (Creeb uh *This*-ghyll)
Starting Point: Pen y Pass car park at the top of Llanberis Pass, GR 647556. There is a charge for parking.
Distance: 6 miles / 9.6 kilometres. **Ascent:** 2306 ft / 706 metres
Estimated Time: 4-7 hours

Route: Garnedd Ugain is the highest but one of Wales' mountains and the view from its summit is stunning – including an exceptionable view of Snowdon itself. Furthermore, three of the popular routes up Snowdon pass within a few minutes' easy walk of its summit. For all that, Garnedd Ugain is largely ignored by the vast majority of walkers who are intent on reaching the summit of the highest mountain in Wales and it is doubtful whether anyone ever visits the mountain for its own sake. If you follow the directions given for Snowdon up to the standing stone at Bwlch Glas, you can reach the summit of Garnedd Ugain easily by turning right and heading north-east to its triangulation point. (Many walkers approach Garnedd Ugain from Crib Goch and continue to Snowdon and many then continue to Y Lliwedd to complete the "Snowdon Horseshoe".)

◀ Garnedd Ugain

Mountain: Y Lliwedd, 2946 ft / 898 m (17)

Map: OS 115, OL 17: GR 622533
Translation: The Hue (or possibly The Troop)
Pronunciation: Uh *Llee*-weth
Starting Point: Pen y Pass car park at the top of Llanberis Pass, GR 647556. There is a charge for parking.
Distance: 5 miles / 8 kilometres. **Ascent:** 1768 ft / 539 metres
Estimated Time: 3-5 hours

Route: Take the wide track – the Miners' Track – which leaves the car park southwards. In about a mile (1.6 kilometres), where the track takes a sharp right turn by Llyn Llydaw, leave it and take a path ahead of you towards a prominent green building. The path follows the shore of the llyn at first but soon begins to climb south-south-west over rocky ground which steepens as you ascend. On the ridge, the path turns south-west and reaches Lliwedd Bach. Here it turns again and follows the cliff edge to the two separate tops which are a clear feature of Y Lliwedd from a distance. The far top (west) is the higher one. Y Lliwedd is often visited as the final peak in the Snowdon Horseshoe – which includes Crib Goch, Garnedd Ugain and Snowdon itself – and because of its steep slopes there is no easy way off the mountain and back to the starting point other than to return the way you came. However, the bus which circles the Snowdon massif in summer could be used to avoid returning by the ascent route. If you carry on down the steep north-west ridge of Y Lliwedd, the path brings you to a large cairn. Turn left (south-west) here and this excellent path (Watkin Path) will take you to the main road at Nantgwynant (GR627506).

Y Lliwedd ▶

Mountain: Yr Aran, 2451 ft / 747 m (56)

Map: OS 115, OL 17: GR 604515
Translation: The High Ridge
Pronunciation: Uhr *Are*-ann
Starting Point: Nantgwynant – the car park at the foot of the Watkin Path up Snowdon, GR 629506.
Distance: 4½ miles / 7.2 kilometres. **Ascent:** 2198 ft / 670 metres
Estimated Time: 3-5 hours

Route: From the car park cross the Afon Glaslyn and then cross the main road to the beginning of the Watkin Path up Snowdon. Take this path for about a mile (1.6 kilometres) to a point where it hugs the Afon Cwm Llan – above waterfalls by a ruin below Y Lliwedd – as you pass round the end of Yr Aran's east ridge (GR 621520). Here, a path climbs south-west to reach the route of a former tramway. Turn right along the old tramway and follow it to where it turns north-east by disued tips. From just before this bend (GR 612513), turn left uphill by a stream and climb to the col between Snowdon and Yr Aran (Bwlch Cwm Llan). From the col turn south following a wall which heads initially towards the black cliffs on Yr Aran's north face but soon turns towards the mountain's eastern ridge. Climb the steep stony slopes of the mountain following the wall until it finally levels out by a ladder stile. Then, turn right (south-west) and head for the summit of Yr Aran which is marked by a large cairn. From here, return to the wall and this time follow it to the right, eastwards. After about 0.4 miles (0.64 kilometres), just before the wall bends to the right, a small cairn on the right of the path marks the spot where you should turn left, downhill (GR 614515) and head north-east, skirting an unfenced chasm, and return to the tramway. Having reached the tramway return to the Watkin Path and turn right to return to the starting point.

Map: OS 115, OL 17: GR 556577, GR 587564

Translation: Eilio's Hill, First Hill (or perhaps Hill of the Councillors)

Pronunciation: Moil *Ay*-leeo, Moil Kung-*horr*-eeon

Starting Point: Llanberis. There is a large car park by Llyn Padarn.

Distance: 9 miles / 14.4 kilometres. **Ascent:** 3192 ft / 973 metres

Estimated Time: 5-8 hours

Route: From the village of Llanberis, take the road to the Youth Hostel. The road climbs from the village and ends near a house. Where the tarmac road ends, go left along a track for just a few metres. Now, cross the stream and the open land on your right, and head for the north-east ridge of Moel Eilio (Braich y Foel). Climb steep grassy slopes to attain the ridge itself and follow the ridge fence to the summit of Moel Eilio with its extensive and varied panorama. Moel Cynghorion can be seen just over two miles (3.2 kilometres) away in the south-east, but it is

Moel Eilio

Snowdon that draws the eye. A very pleasant walk over easy, grassy slopes takes you over Foel Gron and Foel Goch and there then follows a steeper descent south to the col below Moel Cynghorion (Bwlch Maesgwm, GR 573558). From here, climb the gentle slopes of Moel Cynghorion to reach the small cairn on its summit. Return to Bwlch Maesgwm and turn right (north) along the track which takes you back to the house at the end of the tarmac road and down to Llanberis.

4. Nantlle and Beddgelert

To THE WEST of the Snowdon massif, in the Nantlle valley and near the villages of Rhyd-ddu and Beddgelert, lie a number of mountains with great visual appeal and which offer wonderful panoramic views. Although the mountains of the Nantlle Ridge are not very high, the route along the ridge is varied and truly memorable — especially if you walk east-to-west towards the sea — and it offers a rare opportunity in Wales to stay high almost all day. It is also narrow and rocky in places, which adds to the excitement. Across the Nantlle valley you will see Craig y Bera, the forbidding rocky south face of Mynydd Mawr, which stands apart from the other mountains in this area. Moel Hebog, the very impressive peak which dominates the village of Beddgelert, throws down a ridge which invites you to climb it.

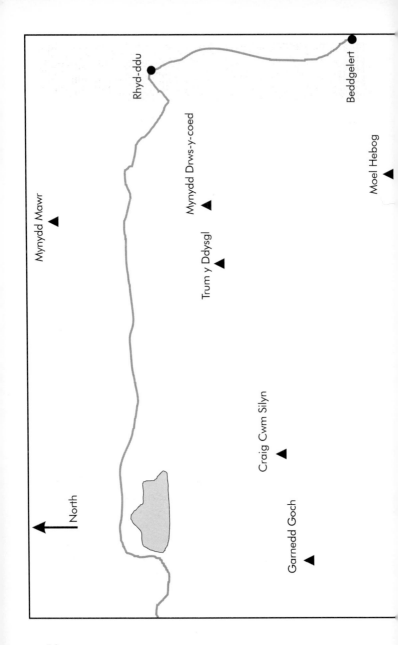

North

Mynydd Mawr

Rhyd-ddu

Mynydd Drws-y-coed

Trum y Ddysgl

Craig Cwm Silyn

Garnedd Goch

Moel Hebog

Beddgelert

50

Mountain: Mynydd Drws-y-coed, 2280 ft / 695 m (76); Trum y Ddysgl, 2326 ft / 709 m (71); Craig Cwm Silyn, 2408 ft / 734 m (59); Garnedd Goch, 2297 ft / 700 m (74)

Map: OS 115, OL 17: GR 549518, GR 545516, GR 525503, GR 511495

Translation: The Mountain of the Wooded Gap, The Ridge of the Dish, The Rock of Silyn's Valley, Red Cairn

Pronunciation: *Mun*-eathe Drooss uh Coid, Trim uh *This*-ghyll, *Cra*-eeg Coom *Sil*-yn, *Garn*-eth Goch

Starting Point: Rhyd-Ddu, GR 572525. Car park.

Distance: 11 miles / 17.2 kilometres. **Ascent:** 3117 ft / 950 metres

Estimated Time: 5-9 hours

Route: It is certainly worth trying to walk the whole of the Nantlle Ridge – all the way from Y Garn in the east to Mynydd y Graig Goch in the west – if time and the strength of the party permits, but in order to return to the starting point the ridge will have to be walked in both directions or a car will be needed at either end. Another possibility is to divide the walk described below into two separate walks, tackling Mynydd Drws-y-coed and Trum y Ddysgl on one walk and Craig Cwm Silyn and Garnedd Goch on another. The hills of the Nantlle Ridge are not particularly high but to walk it in both directions does involve a considerable amount of descent and reascent.

Opposite the car park entrance at Rhyd-Ddu there is a gate. Go through it and cross the field beyond on a slate path. On reaching the house called Tal-y-Llyn, turn left and cross the bridge over the Afon Gwyrfai. Follow the path to the road from Rhyd-Ddu to Nantlle. Turn left immediately along a bridleway which heads down to the south-west. Having crossed a stream, the path to Y Garn can be seen making its way up towards a stile. Once at this stile, you will see a large rock ahead of you with two white painted arrows. Immediately beyond this rock the path divides into two. Go right over steep ground directly towards Y Garn. From its summit, follow a rocky path south to reach Mynydd Drws-y-coed. From here follow the cliff edge and climb to the summit of Trum y Ddysgl to the west. Now turn south-west to reach a narrow ridge beyond which lies the summit of Mynydd Tal-y-mignedd with its tower. From the summit of Mynydd Tal-y-mignedd the path heads off almost due south initially and then takes you down a steep slope south-west to the col below Craig Cwm Silyn (Bwlch Dros-Bern). Once across the col, the route you need climbs up through the rocks ahead to the summit of Craig Cwm Silyn (a short detour along the path to the right may offer an easier initial approach to the rocks). From the summit of Craig Cwm Silyn, it is worth crossing over to the west to look down at Llynnau Cwm Silyn and the splendid rock face of Craig Cwm Silyn before turning south-west to pick up the wall which leads to the summit of Garnedd-goch.

If you decide to tackle the Nantlle Ridge in two separate journeys in the manner suggested above – or if you merely wish to vary the return journey to Rhyd-ddu – you could follow the south ridge of Trum y Ddysgl until you reach the forest and follow the forest edge to the path at Bwlch-y-Ddwy-Elor (GR 553505). Turn left (north-east) to return to Rhyd-ddu.

Craig y Bera, Mynydd Mawr

Map: OS 115, OL 17: GR 525503, GR 511495
Translation: The Rock of Silyn's Valley, Red Cairn
Pronunciation: Craeeg Coom *Sil*-yn, *Garn*-eth Goch
Starting Point: Two miles (3.2 kilometres) east of the village of Llanllyfni, at the end of the road which leads to Cwm Silyn, GR 496511. There is room for a number of vehicles beyond the gate.
Distance: 5 miles / 8 kilometres. **Ascent:** 1542 ft / 470 metres
Estimated Time: 3-5 hours

Route: Take the path east to Cwm Silyn. Before reaching the southern end of the first lake, climb south-west over grassy slopes avoiding the hidden sheer cliff face (Clogwyn y Cysgod) which encircles the head of the cwm. Follow the cliff edge round to the east and head for the cairn on the summit of Craig Cwm Silyn. From the summit turn south-west and aim for the wall which leads to the summit of Garnedd Goch. From the summit follow another wall – north-west this time – on its western side back down towards the starting point.

Mynydd Mawr

Map: OS 115, OL 17: GR 565469
Translation: Hill of the Hawk
Pronunciation: Moil *Hebb*-ogg
Starting Point: Beddgelert – car park, GR 588481.
Distance: 4 miles / 7.2 kilometres. **Ascent:** 2428 ft / 740 metres
Estimated Time: 3-5 hours

Route: Walk from the car park back to the main road. Turn right along the road between the houses and the hotel. Where the road bends left to go behind the hotel, turn right and go through the gate ahead, ignoring the public footpath sign. Follow the track ahead of you which, after about a hundred metres, trends left to pass through a gap in a stone wall. Once through the gap, turn immediately right and take the path between two walls which soon bends left and brings you out onto the road leading south-west towards Cwm Cloch. Turn left along this road. It passes through some tall trees following a stream and reaches a house called Cwm Cloch Canol. Opposite this house is a stile by a ruin and the path to Moel Hebog can be seen crossing flat, wet ground towards the mountain's north-east ridge, which is the route of ascent. On the ridge itself the path turns south-west, climbing steep grassy slopes in the direction of the rocks below the summit ridge. The ground becomes more stony as you gain height and just below the rocks the path turns right to reach the northern ridge of the mountain. Here it turns left towards the grassy summit where there is a triangulation point and a wall.

Mountain: Mynydd Mawr, 2264 ft / 690 m (78)

Map: OS 115, OL 17: GR 540546
Translation: Big Mountain
Pronunciation: *Mun*-eathe *Ma*-oor
Starting Point: Rhyd-Ddu, GR 572525. Car park.
Distance: 6 ½ miles / 10.4 kilometres. **Ascent:** 1850 ft / 564 metres
Estimated Time: 3-6 hours

Route: From the car park, walk through the village of Rhyd-Ddu and turn left along the B4418 to Nantlle. Having passed the houses at Cefn Cwellyn, turn right along a forest road, immediately after the speed restriction signs at the edge of the village. The road rises gradually at first and then levels out. After about three quarters of a mile (1.2 kilometres), when you have just passed the southern end of Llyn Cwellyn which you can see below you through the trees, Mynydd Mawr comes into sight once more above the slope on your left where the trees have recently been cleared. At this point, the road crosses a path (GR 564541) whose right branch can be seen going down through the trees. The left branch, which leads up left to the mountain, may not be immediately clear but it follows the edge of the trees still left standing and climbs to the ridge. Cross the stile over the fence on the ridge where the trees end. Turn right and follow the edge of the plantation and then climb steeply up the grassy eastern ridge of Mynydd Mawr (Foel Rudd). From here, a clear path climbs gradually above the dramatic rocks of Craig y Bera before heading north to climb the grassy upper slopes of the mountain to reach the summit.

5. Blaenau Ffestiniog

MOEL SIABOD can be seen clearly when the mountains of Snowdonia come into view for the first time as you drive west along the straight sections of the A5 past Pentrefoelas and head for the busy tourist village of Betws-y-coed. As you continue past the Swallow Falls and approach Capel Curig it suddenly reappears and its seemingly vast bulk dominates the view as it rises above the village and the campsites. From here, you would hardly think that there is an easy route to its summit. Moel Siabod is, without doubt, the most striking and interesting mountain in this mixed group of mountains. It seems a rather isolated peak, particularly when seen from the east like this, but its western flanks extend to the high expanse above the village of Blaenau Ffestiniog where there are a number of far less striking mountains. These other mountains are normally reached from the Blaenau Ffestiniog side and are, generally speaking, grassy and easy to climb. A little further west lie Cnicht (the so-called Matterhorn of Wales), Moelwyn Mawr and Moelwyn Bach, whose appeal is a great deal more obvious.

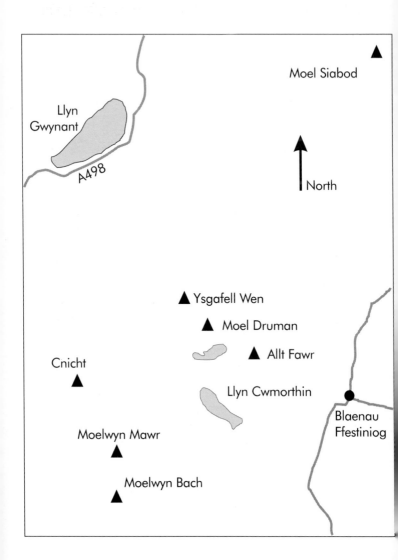

Moel Siabod

Llyn Gwynant

A498

North

Ysgafell Wen

Moel Druman

Allt Fawr

Cnicht

Llyn Cwmorthin

Blaenau Ffestiniog

Moelwyn Mawr

Moelwyn Bach

Map: OS 115 and 124, OL 17 and 18: GR 645466
Translation: Knight
Pronunciation: Cneecht
Starting Point: The village of Croesor – car park, GR 631447.
Distance: 6 miles / 9.6 kilometres. **Ascent:** 1745 ft / 532 metres
Estimated Time: 3-5 hours

Route: Leave the car park and turn right along the road, crossing the
Afon Croesor and passing through the village. Go along the road until
you reach two gates. Go through the gate ahead of you and follow the
track through the trees. Having left the trees, the path divides into two.
Turn right. This path will take you all the way to the summit which
now reappears before you. At a sheep fold the path divides once more.
Turn right again. The path makes its way onto the ridge of the mountain
and proceeds upwards along it towards the summit rocks, where a little
scrambling is necessary. From the summit, either return the way you
came or follow the path north-east along the ridge until you are opposite
the southern end of Llyn yr Adar. Here a substantial stone cairn marks
another path. Turn right (south-east) along this path and cross the Afon
Cwm y Foel. Follow the river's east bank down to the llyn below (Llyn
Cwm-y-foel, GR 655466). Keep well above the rocks which rise from
the llyn until you reach the dam at its southern end. Cross the dam and
turn left to pick up a path which crosses Cnicht's slopes and descends
gradually to the valley floor of Cwm Croesor. Cross the flat grassy area
to reach a bridge near a ruin (GR 642455). A track leads south-east
along the valley. Follow this until a tarmac road is reached near a
farmhouse. Take the road back to the village of Croesor.

Mountain: Moelwyn Bach, 2329 ft / 710 m (70); Moelwyn Mawr, 2526 ft / 770 m (44)

Map: OS 115 and 124, OL 17 and 18: GR 660437, GR 658449
Translation: Little White Hill, Big White Hill
Pronunciation: *Moil*-win Baach, *Moil*-win *Ma*-oor.
Starting Point: The village of Croesor – car park, GR 631447.
Distance: 5½ miles / 8.8 kilometres. **Ascent:** 2438 ft / 743 metres
Estimated Time: 3-5 hours

Route: Leave the car park and turn left along the main road. Follow the road for a little over half a mile (about a kilometre). Having crossed the Afon Maesgwm the road heads for a forest. Leave the road and take a track which comes into view on the left before you reach the forest. Head across open ground for the far corner of the forest where a wall is crossed. Take the grassy west ridge of Moelwyn Bach all the way to the summit. To the north, there is a dangerous, hidden cliff face and from

Moelwyn Bach and Moelwyn Mawr

the summit cairn you should first descend east and then take a narrow path which heads for Moelwyn Mawr. When wet, this path can be treacherous and in its upper reaches, in particular, care is needed. The path improves as it descends towards the col below Moelwyn Mawr (Bwlch Stwlan). From here, climb steeply through rocks to cross Craigysgafn; the grassy upper slopes of Moelwyn Mawr will then come into view once more. There is a triangulation point on the summit, right on the cliff edge. From the summit, a grassy ridge can be seen heading north towards Llyn Croesor. Descend this ridge to reach a path which heads west towards Cwm Croesor where the road back to the village is reached.

Map: OS 115, OL 17: GR 705546

Translation: Barren Hill

Pronunciation: Moil *Shabb*-odd

Starting Point: About a mile (1.6 kilometres) south-east of the village of Capel Curig – by Pont Cyfyng, GR 734572 or in a lay-by on the A5, GR 735571.

Distance: 6 miles / 9.6 kilometres. **Ascent:** 2369 ft / 722 metres

Estimated Time: 3-5 hours

Route: From the A5, cross Pont Cyfyng. Ignore the public footpath on the right. Take the next turning on the right, a tarmac road which climbs steeply through trees. This road actually goes all the way to the north-east ridge of Moel Siabod but a diversion has been created at the first bend to avoid a farmyard. Having rejoined the road, above the farmyard, turn left and go through a gate. Further on a second gate is reached. As you approach the mountain, the ground levels out and immediately before reaching a third gate leave the road and cross rough ground on the right to reach a conspicuous stile over the fence below the mountain ridge. Follow this long ridge to the summit. The level summit ridge turns out to be long and rocky. The rocks can be awkward in places and some may prefer to take an easier route – though it is much less fun – along a narrow path through short grass a little below the rocky ridge on the north side of the mountain. The actual summit is at the far end of the ridge and is marked by a triangulation point. There is a stone shelter nearby.

Moel Siabod

Mountain: Ysgafell Wen, 2205 ft / 672 m (93); Moel Druman, 2218 ft / 676 m (90); Allt Fawr, 2290 ft / 698 m (75)

Map: OS 115, OL 17: GR 667481, GR 672476, GR 682475
Translation: White Ledge, Hill of the Ridges, Great Slope
Pronunciation: Usk-*av*-ell When, Moil *Drim*-ann, Allt-*va*-oor
Starting Point: Tanygrisiau near Blaenau Ffestiniog. Car park, GR 682452.
Distance: 6 miles / 9.6 kilometres. **Ascent:** 2067 ft / 630 m
Estimated Time: 3-6 hours

Route: From the car park, cross back to the east side of the Afon Cwmorthin and turn left along the road northwards to Cwmorthin itself. Where the tarmac road ends, go through the gate and up the steep, stony road. As the road levels out, a bridge is reached with a public footpath sign at a spot which has been landscaped. Either cross the river at this point or continue on the same side until you reach Llyn Cwmorthin where there is a footbridge. The road skirts the western shore of the llyn and after about half a mile (0.8 kilometres) turns left and begins to climb south-west below a rocky ridge (Clogwyn Brith) towards an old quarry. The road ends once the level ground of the old quarry is reached. Turn sharp right here and head north towards Llyn Cwm Corsiog. You will see a cairn and a faint path heading off over wet moorland. As you pass Llyn Cwm Corsiog, with Cnicht in view once more to the west, the path branches into two. From here, ignoring both paths, you could in fact head off across the rocky moorland straight towards the summit of Ysgafell Wen – the 672 height spot over half a mile away (1 kilometre) north-north-east – or you could take the path to the right which heads for Llyn Coch in the north-east. From the far end of the llyn, a clear path follows old fence posts north past Llyn Terfyn to the foot of the rocks below the summit of Ysgafell Wen. A small cairn on the rocks marks the highest point. From the summit, head south-east along a path which passes Llyn Terfyn and Llyn Coch and then climbs over the summit ridge of Moel Druman where a short detour left will bring you to the unmarked summit. The path then continues past Llyn Conglog and over Allt Fawr. Once again, a detour left is needed to reach the summit, which is marked by a cairn on a low rock outcrop. Return to the path. The aim now is to descend the ridge south-east, avoiding the cliffs of Allt Fawr in the east and Allt y Ceffylau in the west. Follow the left side of the electric fence which at first heads south-west and soon turns south-east. As the ground levels out, a gate is reached where the fence turns sharp right. Go through the gate and descend grassy slopes to Llyn Cwmorthin where there is a stile. Once over the stile, go through the quarry and pick up the road back to Tanygrisiau.

6. Arenig

HIGH ABOVE BALA, on either side of the main road to Trawsfynydd and overlooking Llyn Celyn, stand Arenig Fawr and her little sister Arenig Fach. Arenig Fawr is undoubtedly the queen of this group of mountains. As you climb from Bala towards Llyn Celyn, its large, rocky eastern face dominates the scenery. From this direction, the rocky eastern face of Arenig Fach also looks very impressive — which indeed it is — but it soon disappears from view and the mountain can otherwise seem a rather dull grassy hill. Not far away, but rather obscured, is the much less striking Carnedd y Filiast whose central location affords views of Snowdonia, the Clwydian range, the Berwyn range and much more besides. Moel Llyfnant is overshadowed by Arenig Fawr and is seldom visited for its own sake. To the south lies Rhobell Fawr which is usually reached from the Bala-Dolgellau road.

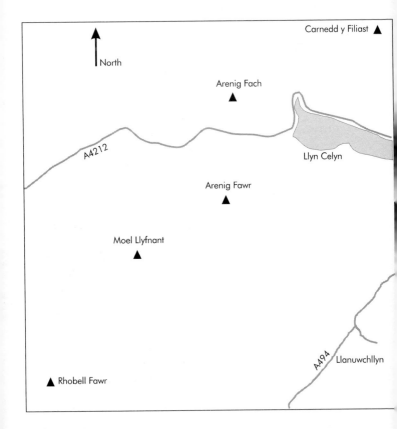

North

Carnedd y Filiast ▲

Arenig Fach
▲

A4212

Llyn Celyn

Arenig Fawr
▲

Moel Llyfnant
▲

A494 Llanuwchllyn

▲ Rhobell Fawr

Map: OS 124 or 125, OL 18: GR 820416
Translation: Lesser Upland
Pronunciation: Are-*enn*-ig Vaach
Starting Point: The A4212 – opposite the road and public footpath which go down to the farm of Rhyd-y-fen, GR 826400. There is room to park a few cars on the northern side of the road.
Distance: 2-3 miles / 3-5 kilometres. **Ascent:** 1122 ft / 342 metres
Estimated Time: 1½-3 hours

Route: Go through the gate and pass between two rows of stones for about fifteen metres until you are beyond the end of the stone wall which climbs the slope. Walk up the steep grassy slopes ahead, crossing two collapsed stone walls. There is now an obvious rock outcrop just ahead – pass it on the right and then go through a third wall. Turn immediately left along a path which follows this wall. Ahead, the ground on the right rises and once you have passed between the wall and the rise, turn uphill once more. An obvious hollow in the ground trends slightly left uphill towards a gate in the uppermost wall. Once through the gate, turn right and follow the path through the heather for about 100 metres. Immediately before reaching the large boulder in the heather the path turns left uphill once again. Shortly afterwards it trends to the right over a short rise where the soil is exposed and heads for Y Foel – the top of the south ridge of Arenig Fach. However, instead of leading to the cairn at the summit of Y Foel, the path heads across a heathery plateau towards the summit of Arenig Fach and comes to an abrupt end half way along this plateau. Continue in the same direction, over rough ground and up a slope from the top of which the triangulation point and stone shelter of the summit of Arenig Fach come into view. Before heading back, it is worth heading east to see the mountain's most striking – and most unexpected – feature, the rocky eastern face and the view down to Llyn Arenig Fach. For those with a head for heights, there is a broad, flat rock on the cliff edge.

Map: OS 124 or 125, OL 18: GR 827369
Translation: Greater Upland
Pronunciation: Are-*enn*-ig *Va*-oor
Starting Point: Slightly east of Pont Rhyd-y-fen, the bridge over the Afon Tryweryn, GR 823393. There is room to park beside the road.
Distance: 5-6 miles / 8-9.6 kilometres. **Ascent:** 1673 ft / 510 metres
Estimated Time: 2-5 hours

Route: Follow the road which heads off south-west near the former railway line. Gradually this road changes to a narrow path. After about half a mile (0.8 kilometres) the path turns southwards and passes an old quarry, leaving the course of the old railway. In another half a mile, a gate in a wall is reached. Stay this side of the wall. Turn left uphill and follow the wall – which later becomes a fence and then a mere succession of fence posts – up the north-west ridge of the mountain and then proceed along its long flattish top all the way to the summit itself, where there is a triangulation point and a memorial stone. (On the north-west ridge, to avoid any possible confusion if you decide to return by the ascent route, notice that for part of the way there are actually *two* walls). The return journey can be varied by setting off south until you are beyond the rocks below the summit and then turning west to descend to the path which will take you north, through the ruins of Amnodd-wen, and back to the starting point.

Arenig Fawr

Map: OS 124 or 125, OL 18: GR 808352
Translation: Hill of the Smooth Stream (or Valley)
Pronunciation: Moil *Llove*-nant
Starting Point: Slightly east of Pont Rhyd-y-fen, the bridge over the Afon Tryweryn, GR 823393. There is room to park beside the road.
Distance: 7 miles / 11.2 kilometres. **Ascent:** 1345 ft / 410 metres
Estimated Time: 3-6 hours

Route: Follow the road which heads off south-west near the former railway line. Gradually this road becomes a narrow path. After about half a mile (0.8 kilometres) the path turns southwards and passes an old quarry, leaving the course of the old railway. Continue for about three quarters of a mile (1.2 kilometres) until you reach the old ruins of Amnodd-wen. Immediately beyond, the path forks. Go to the right through trees until you reach the ruins of Amnodd-bwll. In front of the old house take the path left and go through the gate by the stream. Now leave the track and head left through old sheepfolds and up to the grassy north ridge of Moel Llyfnant. Follow the ridge to the summit, immediately before which a wall and fence meet. To vary the return journey, go back to where the wall and fence meet and then head down east on grassy slopes and follow the foot of the mountain back to Amnodd-bwll.

Map: OS 124, OL 23: GR 787256
Translation: Big Saddle
Pronunciation: *Rhob*-ell *Va*-oor
Starting Point: About 3 miles (4.8 kilometres) north of the village
of Rhydymain – on the forest road below the eastern slopes of
Rhobell Fawr, GR 798255. (The map shows a house called Tŷ-
newydd-y-mynydd a little to the north, though nothing at all
remains of it.) Park at the roadside.
Distance: 2 miles / 3.2 kilometres. **Ascent:** 833 ft / 254 metres
Estimated Time: 1-3 hours

Route: A look at the map reveals that you have just crossed two streams
to reach the starting point. Immediately north of the two streams, at
GR 798255, a wall climbs north-west over the rocky slopes of Rhobell
Fawr. This wall – which has an old fence on top of it and a new fence
running alongside it – leads almost to the top of the mountain and you
can follow either side of it. If you choose the right side (north) do as
follows: follow the wall and old fence until you reach another wall.
Cross this second wall and proceed in the same direction, still following
the original wall, until you reach a third wall. Now, go over the fallen
wall on your left and follow the good wall until you reach a stile near
the summit, which is a grassy knoll with a triangulation point on top. If
you choose to walk on the left side of the original wall, follow it until
you reach a second wall. At this point, you will need to turn left to
reach a stile. From the top of this stile, you can see the triangulation
point on the summit. Walk straight towards it and you will reach a stile
in the wall immediately below the summit.

Map: OS 125, OL 18: GR 871446
Translation: Cairn of the Greyhound Bitch
Pronunciation: *Carn*-eth uh *Vill*-yast
Starting Point: By Llyn Celyn – about 5 miles (8 kilometres) from
Bala on the A4212 to Trawsfynydd. There is room to park in a lay-by
on the north side of the road, GR861411.
Distance: 6-7 miles / 9.6-12.8 kilometres. **Ascent:** 1325 ft / 404
metres
Estimated Time: 3-5 hours

Route: From the lay-by beside the main road, take the track into
the forest. Almost immediately, you reach an open area in the forest
where vehicles turn and about a hundred metres beyond this point a
path to the right heads off uphill to the forest edge. Take this path
and when you emerge from the trees pass below the electricity cables
and follow a track north. Below the slopes of Foel Boeth this track
suddenly turns east. It could be followed all the way to the summit of
Carnedd y Filiast but it loses height for about half a mile (0.8
kilometres) until it crosses the Nant y Coed below the slopes of
Brottos. So, leave the track at the point where it turns east and walk
straight through the heather to the top of Foel Boeth. From there,
descend north to the col below Llechwedd-llyfn, climb to the top of
the mountain and follow its grassy summit until a fence is reached.
Turn right and follow the fence east for about a mile (1.6 kilometres)
to reach the triangulation point on the summit of Carnedd y Filiast.
To vary the journey back, you could follow the track which you left
below Foel Boeth. From the triangulation point the track actually
heads north initially, but soon turns sharply to head back to the
forest.

7. Berwyn

THE BUSY A5 BRINGS weekend and summer walkers who are naturally keen to see the summits of Snowdonia, and as they drive from Llangollen to Corwen — through Owain Glyndŵr country — they are not likely to be impressed by what little they see of the Berwyn range. They may also have heard tales of trudging through endless miles of heather over rather dull hills. And indeed, if they were to take the mountain road from Bala to Llangynog in Powys, to get a better view than that afforded by the A5, their impressions might well be confirmed. To the left are the range's highest peaks — Moel Sych, Cadair Berwyn and Cadair Bronwen — in a low-lying row, and to the right a vast expanse of heather stretches as far as the eye can see. The appeal of these hills, to a large extent, is their sense of isolation and the demands they make of walkers. But there is another side to the main hills in this group and if you approach them from the east — from Glyn Ceiriog or the Tanat Valley — the view is quite different. The rocky face of Craig Berwyn is quite unexpected and the view from the summit reveals the lonely Llyn Lluncaws, whilst nearby is the spectacular waterfall of Pistyll Rhaeadr, one of the seven wonders of Wales.

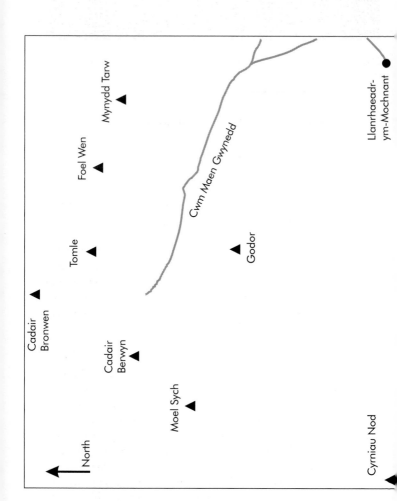

North

Cadair Bronwen
Tomle
Foel Wen
Mynydd Tarw
Cadair Berwyn
Moel Sych
Cwm Maen Gwynedd
Godor
Cyrniau Nod
Llanrhaeadr-ym-Mochnant

Mountain: Mynydd Tarw, 2234 ft / 681 m (86); Foel Wen, 2267 ft / 691 m (77); Tomle, 2434 ft / 742 m (57); Cadair Bronwen 2575 ft / 785 m (41); Cadair Berwyn, 2723 ft / 830 m (28); Moel Sych 2713 ft / 827 m (29); Godor, 2228 ft / 679 m (88)

Map: OS 125, P 826: GR 113324, GR 099334, GR 085335, GR 077346, GR 072324, GR 066318, GR 095307

Translation: Bull Mountain, White Hill, Heaps, Branwen's Seat, Berwyn's Seat, Dry Hill, (?) Plateau

Pronunciation: *Muhn*-ith *Tar*-oo, Voil *When*, *Tom*-leh, *Cad*-ire *Bron*-when, *Cad*-ire *Bear*-win, Moil-Seech, *Godd*-awr

Starting Point: Cwm Maen Gwynedd, by the telephone kiosk, GR 118308. There is parking space for two or three cars by the bridge over the stream below.

Distance: 11 miles / 17.6 kilometres. **Ascent:** 2657 ft / 810 metres

Estimated Time: 4-8 hours

Route: Go up the lane by the telephone kiosk and through the farmyard at Maes. Where the lane bends right, turn left (north-north-west) through the farther of the two gates. Climb through the field to another gate and go through it. Turn immediately right, following the trees to a track which now climbs to the corner of a large plantation. Follow the edge of the forest over steep ground to reach the stone shelter on the summit of Mynydd Tarw. From there, follow the fence west for a mile (1.6 kilometres) to reach the summit of Foel Wen. The highest point is on the north side of the fence. Continue north-west along the fence and it will lead you to the summit of Tomle which is marked by a small cairn of white stones. From there, the fence is followed down to the col below Cadair Berwyn where, until recently, stood Maen Gwynedd – a standing stone (now recumbent) some eight feet long – on an ancient track through the hills. Go through the gate and follow this ancient track west to reach another gate at Bwlch Maen Gwynedd. Go through this second gate and turn right to follow a clear path north over grassy slopes to the summit of Cadair Bronwen with its large cairn. From here, return to Bwlch Maen Gwynedd. You could cut the journey in half at this point and leave the second half for another day by doing the following – go back through the gate and return along the ancient track to the first gate near the fallen Maen Gwynedd. Go through the gate there and descend south-south-east to the tarmac road in Cwm Maen Gwynedd which will take you back to the starting point.

If you wish to complete the walk in one day, leave Bwlch Maen Gwynedd and follow the fence which climbs south up the slopes of Cadair Berwyn. On the top of the slope the fence turns left and joins another fence where there is a gate and a stile. Cross the stile and just ahead of you is a path which follows the cliff edge. Turn right along it and proceed to the summit of Cadair Berwyn – not the triangulation point which you see first, but the rocks further on to the south, shortly beyond a stone shelter. From the summit, with its view down Cwm Maen Gwynedd and to Llyn Lluncaws, walk south-west over short grass for three quarters of a mile (1.2 kilometres) to reach the summit of Moel Sych where there is a large cairn and where three fences meet. Now walk back down towards Cadair Berwyn and just as the land begins to rise again turn right and take a narrow path which crosses the east face of the mountain to the fence on the south-east ridge above Llyn Lluncaws. Cross the small stile and follow the fence on its northern side. The vegetation and terrain can be difficult here, and where the path veers off right it is best to hold your direction despite the difficulties. The fence soon comes back to meet you. Now follow the fence to the highest point of Godor which is marked by a small cairn of white stones at a point immediately before three fences meet. The aim now is to descend east along the ridge where grassy slopes make the going much easier. Aim for a sheepfold at the bottom of a field near a small copse. Two fields beyond this a track is reached. Turn left to reach the tarmac road. Turn left again to return to the telephone kiosk.

Map: OS 125, P 825: GR 989279

Translation: Marked Cones (or possibly Cairns)

Pronunciation: *Kern*-ya Node

Starting Point: Bwlch Hirnant, the col on the minor road from Bala to Llyn Efyrnwy – about 6 miles (9.6 kilometres) south of Bala, GR 946273. There is room to park at the side of the road.

Distance: 7 miles / 11.2 kilometres. **Ascent:** 745 ft / 227 metres

Estimated Time: 3-5 hours

Route: From the col, take the forest road which climbs north-east towards Penllyn Forest, which it serves. After about three miles (4.8 kilometres) the flat top of Foel Cedig is reached. From there, the road continues east and then takes a sharp turn north. Leave the road at this turning, and cross rough ground south to reach a fence. Turn right along the fence until you reach another fence going left (south-south-east). Follow the east side of this fence to reach the summit of Cyrniau Nod which is at the far end of the ridge. There is a small cairn. From this point, heather-covered moorland extends in all directions and this is certainly one of the loneliest mountains in Wales.

Cadair Berwyn

8. Aran

As YOU TRAVEL west towards Bala, the long north ridge of Aran Benllyn seems to fall abruptly into the far end of Llyn Tegid, above which it rises impressively. But as your journey towards Dolgellau continues, the illusion is exposed and the ridge appears far more gentle — which is as well, for this is the route the path takes to the summit. From Aran Benllyn a long, high connecting ridge leads to the sister summit of Aran Fawddwy. This sister peak is actually best viewed from the south — from the hills above Machynlleth or from the summits of Pumlumon or Cadair Idris — and it is usually approached from Cwm Cywarch above Dinas Mawddwy. Although the summit and upper slopes of Aran Fawddwy are clad in stone, in general the mountains of this group are grassy and give excellent walking and superb views. Disagreement about access matters in this area in the past have led to the establishment of courtesy paths which are shown on maps located at various strategic points along the paths.

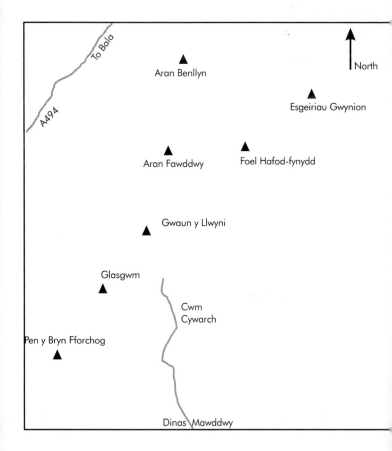

Mountain: Aran Benllyn, 2904 ft / 885 m (20)

Map: OS 124 or 125, OL18 and OL 23: GR 867243
Translation: High Ridge above the Head of the Lakes
Pronunciation: *Are*-ann *Ben*-llin
Starting Point: Llanuwchllyn – the bend in the B4403 by the bridge over the Afon Twrch, GR 880298. There is a car park immediately before the bend.
Distance: 7 miles / 11.2 kilometres. **Ascent:** 2379 ft / 725 metres
Estimated Time: 3-5 hours

Route: By the bridge a map and a sign remind walkers that local landowners have granted permission to use the marked path to the summit of Aran Benllyn. Cross the stile and take the road to a point where it starts to head south. Another stile is now seen on the right, on top of a rise by a cattle grid, and a path heads south-west across fields. Shortly, you need to leave this path too and climb over a hillock taking a path south by another map and sign. This path descends to a flat, wet area and then begins a slow ascent over Moel Ffenigl before climbing the steep slope to the summit of Aran Benllyn. The highest point is on the southern side of the ruined wall, on the cliff edge.

Aran Benllyn

Mountain: Aran Fawddwy, 2969 ft / 905 m (16); Gwaun y Llwyni, 2247 ft / 685 m (83)

Map: OS 124 or 125, OL 23: GR 863224, GR 857205
Translation: The High Ridge of Mawddwy, Moorland of the Bushes
Pronunciation: *Are*-ann *Vow*-thooee, Gwine uh *Lloo*-inee
Starting Point: Cwm Cywarch – about 3 miles (4.8 kilometres) north of Dinas Mawddwy, GR 854185. There is plenty of room to park on the flat area to the left of the road just before it ends.
Distance: 8 miles / 12.8 kilometres. **Ascent:** 2503 ft / 763metres
Estimated Time: 4-6 hours

Route: Walk north along the road until you reach a footbridge where a map and a sign show the way to the top of Aran Fawddwy. Cross the footbridge and take the path which climbs gradually north-east above Hengwm and then turns north below Waun Goch and then north-west up to Drysgol. From the top of Drysgol go west through the narrow gap of Drws Bach and climb rocky slopes along a cairned path to the summit of Aran Fawddwy in the north. There is a triangulation point on the edge of the cliffs above Creiglyn Dyfi. From the summit return south-west along the path to the stile as if you were intending to return to Drws Bach. Instead, follow the fence down to the south-west and as the ground levels out turn left (east), crossing rough ground to reach the cliff edge above Hengwm. Follow the cliff edge southwards and climb the grassy slopes to reach the summit of Gwaun y Llwyni. A tempting ridge invites you back down to Hengwm from here but return instead to the path by the fence. This leads south-west to the col below Glasgwm. Here, turn left (south-east) and take a charming path past a number of small waterfalls back to Cwm Cywarch.

Mountain: Esgeiriau Gwynion, 2201 ft / 671 m (94); Foel Hafod-fynydd, 2260 ft / 689 m (81)

Map: OS 125, OL 23: GR 890236, GR 877227
Translation: White Ridges, Hill of the Mountain Summer Dwelling
Pronunciation: Es-*gay*-ree-I Goo-*in*-eeon, Voil *Have*-odd *Vuhn*-eth
Starting Point: Bwlch y Groes – the pass about 3 miles (4.8 kilometres) north of Llanymawddwy, GR 913233. There is a large car park.
Distance: 7 miles / 11.2 kilometres. **Ascent:** 2067 ft / 630 metres
Estimated Time: 3-5 hours

Route: From the car park follow the north side of the fence for over a mile and a quarter (about 2 kilometres) over rough and boggy ground to reach Llechwedd Du (GR 894224) above the gorge of Ceunant y Briddell. Here, the fence turns north and it can be followed over easier ground all the way to the summit of Esgeiriau Gwynion, where three fences meet. Now follow the fence which descends steeply south-west to the col of Bwlch Sirddyn and follow it across the col and up over steep grassy slopes to the ridge of Foel Hafod-fynydd. On the ridge, the fence turns right and in about half a mile (0.8 kilometres) the summit of Foel Hafod-fynydd is reached – the second cairned hillock. Return east along the ridge and either descend via the fence once more to Bwlch Sirddyn to pick up the track which descends east-south-east or continue east along the ridge and trend left (north) to avoid Ceunant y Briddell and pick up the same track lower down by crossing the stream. The path continues south below Llechwedd Du and eventually emerges onto a tarmac road by the farm of Blaen-pennant. Take the steep road north back to Bwlch y Groes.

Map: OS 124 or 125, OL 23: GR 837195, GR 818179
Translation: Grey Valley, Top of the Forked Hill
Pronunciation: *Glass*-coom, Pen uh Brin *Forch*-og
Starting Point: Cwm Cywarch – about 3 miles (4.8 kilometres) north of Dinas Mawddwy, GR 854185. There is plenty of room to park on the flat area to the left of the road just before it ends.
Distance: 6½ miles / 12.8 kilometres. **Ascent:** 2350 ft / 716 metres
Estimated Time: 3-5 hours

Route: Go north along the road and pass the bridge where there is a sign to show the way up to the Aran ridge. Follow the Afon Cywarch until you reach another bridge by the farm of Blaencywarch (not to be confused with the feature called Blaencywarch on the 1:50 000 map). The path turns left at this bridge and then immediately right by the farm gate. Turn left at a sign which points uphill to Rhydymain and climb steep slopes to leave the valley behind. The path follows a stream through the gap between the rock faces of Craig Cywarch and Creigiau Camddwr. On the col a small lake is reached and you can see the white posts which mark the courtesy path to Aran Fawddwy. Pass the lake and turn left (south) following the fence. Climb the steep grassy slopes of Glasgwm to reach its striking summit cairn. Ahead lies Llyn y Fign. Instead of crossing the stile on the shore of the llyn, follow the fence right. The fence soon turns in the direction of Cadair Idris and the sea before turning once more towards the large forest on the northern slopes of Pen y Bryn Fforchog. Follow the fence to the far end of the forest. Then, cross the stile and follow the upper edge of the forest towards the summit of Pen y Bryn Fforchog. Detour uphill to reach the fence on the grassy summit and cross it to attain the highest point. From the summit, return northwards and as you begin to climb from the hollow below the summit you will see a fire break in the forest (it is marked as a path on the map, GR 818182). Take this path. In about three quarters of a mile (1.2 kilometres) it crosses the Nant y Graig Wen, which flows from Llyn y Fign, and then climbs right before making a gradual descent to a road which leads out of the forest. Turn left along the road, which soon emerges from the trees. Where the road takes a sharp right turn to descend to the valley below, go left along the fence and cross a stile. Then cross the fence which is on your left and turn right along a short plateau to find the rough track which descends steeply to Cwm Cywarch.

9. Rhinog

MANY WALKERS curse the mounains which give this group its name
because of the thick heather intermingled with stones and rocks
which can make walking in this area tiring and tiresome. It is
certainly worth bearing in mind that on terrain such as this a walk
can take much longer than expected. Nor are these mountains easy to
reach when you consider that they are best approached from the
west, along a narrow and winding road to the head of Cwm Nantcol.
These difficulties of terrain and access, however, are rewarded with a
sensation of isolation, and the sea and the Llŷn peninsula provide a
marvellous background. As a group, these mountains are seen to best
advantage from the east — from Moel Llyfnant or Aran Benllyn for
example — and the flat top of Rhinog Fach is easily recognised. The
mountains at the southern end of this range are not covered in
heather and here you can extend your stride.

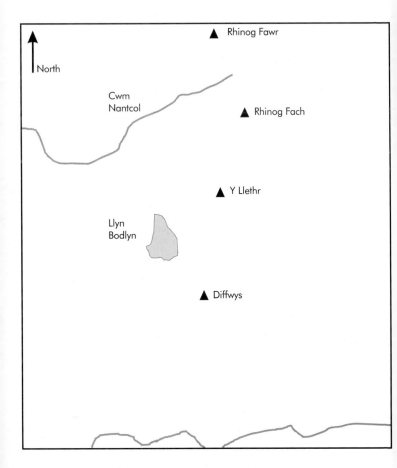

North

▲ Rhinog Fawr

▲ Rhinog Fach

Cwm
Nantcol

▲ Y Llethr

Llyn
Bodlyn

▲ Diffwys

Mountain: Rhinog Fawr, 2362 ft / 720 m (65); Rhinog Fach, 2333 ft / 712 m (69); Y Llethr, 2480 ft / 756 m (50)

Map: OS 124, OL 18: GR 657290, GR 665270, GR 661258
Translation: Greater Threshold, Lesser Threshold, The Steep Slope
Pronunciation: *Rhee*-nog *Va*-oor, *Rhee*-nog Vaach, Uh *Lleth*-uhr
Starting Point: Cwm Nantcol – 5 miles south-east of Harlech. You can park at the road end for a small fee.
Distance: 7 miles / 11.2 kilometres. **Ascent:** 3707 ft / 1130 metres
Estimated Time: 3-6 hours

Route: Follow the lane north to Nantcol. Cross the fields to a stile over a wall. Walk north-east through thick vegetation aiming for the lowest point on the skyline to the left of Rhinog Fawr's south-west ridge. There is no clear path until you turn towards the summit and reach a

wall on the western slopes of the mountain. From the summit, head east at first. Then turn south choosing the easiest route between the rocks to reach Bwlch Drws Ardudwy. If you so wish, you may turn right here (south-west) to return to the starting point. From the col a clear path climbs to the summit of Rhinog Fach. From there, follow the wall east and then south and descend steep slopes to the col. (There is now another opportunity to return to the starting point by following a path from the northern end of Llyn Hywel past Llyn Cwmhosan in the north and down to the path at Bwlch Drws Ardudwy.) Having passed Llyn Hywel, the path deviates from the wall and climbs the steep slopes of Y Llethr to reach the wall once more. Turn right to reach the summit. Return to Llyn Hywel and head north to Llyn Cwmhosan and onwards to Bwlch Drws Ardudwy. There, turn left and take the path back to Cwm Nantcol.

Rhinog Fach with Rhinog Fawr visible in the background

Mountain: Diffwys, 2461 ft / 750 m (54)

Map: OS 124, OL 18: GR 661234
Translation: Precipice
Pronunciation: *Deef*-oois
Starting Point: The end of the lane which goes north from the village of Bont-ddu by the Afon Mawddach. There is space for a number of cars on the left.
Distance: 6 miles / 9.6 kilometres. **Ascent:** 2461 ft / 750 metres
Estimated Time: 3-6 hours

Route: Go through the gate and take the path which heads for the rise on your left (Banc-y-Frân), ignoring the public footpath sign to the right which points to the farm of Hafod-uchaf in the hollow below. A series of white posts leads you towards Braich, the conspicuous grassy ridge which extends towards you. A path takes you between two walls and when you emerge once more keep walking in the same direction (north-north-west) – with a wall to your left – for over a mile (1.6 kilometres) all the way to the top of the ridge. Once there, you reach a stile over another wall. Turn right (north-east) and follow this wall – on either side – over gently rising grass slopes until you reach the rocky slope which leads to the summit. There is a triangulation point on the cliff edge.

10. Cadair Idris

CADAIR IDRIS is one of the best known mountains in Wales. Apart from Snowdon itself, it is the mountain which non-mountaineers are most likely to have heard of. The correct name for the summit is actually Pen y Gadair, though many people now use the name Cadair Idris. In fact the Cadair Idris *massif* extends from Dolgellau to Tal-y-llyn and onwards to the sea, and one can walk several miles on easy, high-level paths with splendid views in all directions. There is considerable variety in the terrain too, from gentle grass slopes to perpendicular rock faces. The cliffs around Llyn Cau are possibly the most striking in all Wales. Add to these features the lakes, boulder fields, ridges, forests, rivers and valleys — not to mention the wonderful panoramic views — and one can see immediately why this area is so popular with walkers. Away from the Cadair Idris *massif*, the other mountains in this group are generally grass-covered and provide good walking and good views, but they are much less frequented.

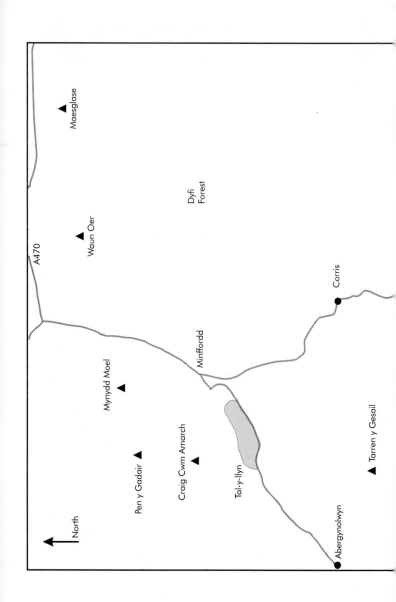

North

Maesglase ▲

Dyfi Forest

A470

Waun Oer ▲

Corris ●

Mynydd Moel ▲

Minffordd

Pen y Gadair ▲

Craig Cwm Amarch ▲

Tal-y-llyn

Tarren y Gesail ▲

Abergynolwyn ●

Mountain: Mynydd Moel, 2831 ft / 863 m (23); Pen y Gadair, 2930 ft / 893 m (18); Craig Cwm Amarch, 2595 ft / 791 m (39)

Map: OS 124, OL 23: GR 728137, GR 711130, GR 711121

Translation: Idris's Seat – Bare Mountain, Top of the Seat, Amarch Valley Rock

Pronunciation: *Cad*-ire Idris, *Muhn*-ith Moil, Pen-uh-*gad*-ire, *Cra*-eeg Coom *Am*-arch

Starting Point: Minffordd – about 4 miles / 6.4 kilometres south of Dolgellau, GR 732115. Dôl Idris car park.

Distance: 5 miles / 8 kilometres. **Ascent:** 2920 ft / 890 metres

Estimated Time: 3-5 hours

Route: From the far end of the car park follow the Cader Idris signs. Having crossed the Nant Cadair the path – called the Minffordd Path – turns right and follows its western bank up through the trees. When you emerge from the trees on this western bank, continue along the path until you are opposite the spot where the forest ends on the other bank. Here, cross the stream and climb a grassy slope north-east, following the upper edge of the forest. A clear path now comes into sight and heads towards Mynydd Moel. The stony path passes through a wall and continues to a stile over a fence besides an old wall. When you reach this stile turn left uphill. There is a path on either side of the fence. Follow the fence up steep heathery slopes to the top of Mynydd Moel. As the ground levels out, you need to be on the right hand side of the fence and there are several stiles available. Trend right, away from the fence, to reach the rocky summit, which is on the cliff edge. From the summit, an easy walk over gentle terrain brings you to Pen y Gadair about a mile away (1.6 kilometres) west-south-west. From Pen y Gadair – where there is a roofed mountain shelter – follow the cliff edge of Craig Cau and climb steeply to the top of Craig Cwm Amarch some three quarters of a mile (1.2 kilometres) south. From here, a good path – the Minffordd path once more – follows the rocky ridge, south-east at first, and descends to the floor of the cwm a little to the east of Llyn Cau. Continue east along the path to reach Nant Cadair and then south to return through the forest.

Craig Cwm Amarch and Pen y Gadair

Mountain: Waun Oer, 2198 ft / 670 m (96); Maesglase, 2211 ft / 674 m (92)

Map: OS 124, OL 23: GR 786148, GR 822152
Translation: Cold Moor, Grey Upland
Pronunciation: *Wa*-een Oir, *Mice*-glass-eh
Starting Point: Bwlch Oerddrws – about 5 miles (8 kilometres) east of the town of Dolgellau. Car park, GR 803170.
Distance: 8½ miles / 13.6 kilometres. **Ascent:** 2539 ft / 774 metres
Estimated Time: 4-7 hours

Route: From the car park, cross the stile and take the path south, which initially follows the western side of the fence and then climbs directly up the steep slopes of Craig y Bwlch. Continue along this path until you reach the level grass ridge above the rocks. On the ridge, the path is joined by a fence and both path and fence run side by side all the way to the flat summit of Cribin Fawr. There, cross the two stiles which are side by side and follow the other side of the fence south-west towards Waun Oer. At the first bend in the fence, where it begins to descend to the col below Waun Oer, note that there is a path off to your left, heading south-east. Once you have visited the summit of Waun Oer you will need to return to this spot and take this path. In the meantime, follow the fence down to the col and climb the steep slope to reach the triangulation point on the summit of Waun Oer. From there, return to the spot mentioned earlier and take the path heading south-east. This path descends gradually to the col below Craig Portas some three quarters of a mile (1.2 kilometres) away. At the col, it finally reaches the fence which has been to your left for some time. The fence climbs the short steep slope of Craig Portas and there turns east. Stay on the southern side of the fence at this point for in the context of the gentle grassy terrain which characterises much of this walk, the vertical cliff which appears suddenly on the other side of this fence can be rather unexpected. (If you do decide to cross to the northern side of the fence, bear in mind that the cliff itself is out of sight and that in places the ground slopes downwards towards it in such a way as to be a real danger, especially if the grass is wet.) Beyond this spot, the fence can be followed north-east to the summit of Maesglase. Return to the top of Craig Portas, follow the fence north-west to the top of Cribin Fawr and from there return the way you came.

Mountain: Tarren y Gesail, 2188 ft / 667 m (99)

Map: OS 124 and 135, OL 23: GR 711059
Translation: Knoll of the Hollow
Pronunciation: *Tar*-ren uh *Guess*-I'll
Starting Point: Abergynolwyn – about 7 miles / 11.2 kilometres
north-east of Tywyn, GR 678069. Village car park.
Distance: 6 miles / 9.6 kilometres. **Ascent:** 2100 ft / 640 metres
Estimated Time: 3-5 hours

Route: From the car park, take the minor road which climbs above
Nant Gwernol in the south-east. After about a mile (1.6 kilometres)
the tarmac road ends and the track ahead branches into two. Take the
grassy track down to the right, staying alongside the fence. As you
approach the old quarry at Bryn Eglwys, the track becomes a narrow
path. This path passes the old quarry and can be very muddy at this
point. When you see a public footpath sign by a stile, turn left and go
up through the trees. The path now turns south-east once more and
emerges from the wood. To the left, on the slopes of Tarren y Gesail,
there is another plantation which hides the summit of the mountain.
The path aims for the bottom of the plantation where it turns left (east)
to reach a gate. From here, you could tackle the steep grassy slopes of
the mountain heading directly for the summit. A more pleasant and
interesting route, however, is to follow the edge of the plantation north
to reach the mountain's south-west ridge which offers splendid views
towards Cadair Idris. There is a triangulation point on the summit of
Tarren y Gesail where two fences meet.

11. Pumlumon

IN MID-WALES there are still places where one can walk for hours and see but few people. The area around Pumlumon is one such place. The mountains in this group, which lie to the east of the Nant-y-Moch reservoir — and especially the lower hills and their adjacent valleys — offer one a chance to wander for many miles, usually in peace. In places, the vegetation can cause difficulties and, especially after heavy rain, some low-lying parts of this area can be treacherous. But the route described below, which takes in all the major summits, is quite straightforward. The sources of two great rivers — the Wye and the Severn — are to be found on the eastern slopes of Pumlumon and it is worth setting aside a little extra time to visit these.

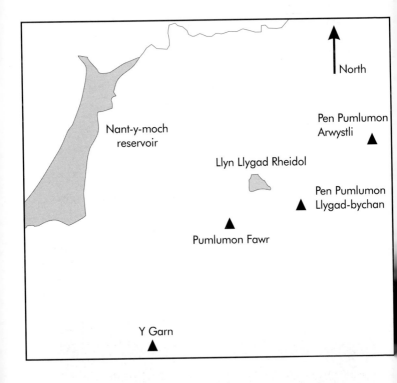

North

Nant-y-moch reservoir

Pen Pumlumon Arwystli ▲

Llyn Llygad Rheidol

Pen Pumlumon Llygad-bychan ▲

Pumlumon Fawr ▲

Y Garn ▲

Mountain: Y Garn, 2244 ft / 684 m (85); Pumlumon Fawr, 2467 ft / 752 m (52); Pen Pumlumon Llygad-bychan, 2385 ft / 727 m (62); Pen Pumlumon Arwystli, 2431 ft / 741 m (58)

Map: OS 135, P 927 and 928: GR 776852, GR 790870, GR 799871, GR 815878

Translation: The Cairn, The Great Five-Peaks Summit, The Five-Peaks Summit of the Small Source, The Five-Peaks Summit in Arwystli

Pronunciation: Uh Garn, Pim-*lim*-on *Va*-oor, Pen Pim-*lim*-on *Llug*-ad *Buch*-an, Pen Pim-*lim*-on Are-*whist*-lee

Starting Point: Nant-y-moch reservoir – where the Nant-y-moch flows into the reservoir, GR 767869. There is room to park at the side of the road.

Distance: 8 miles / 12.8 kilometres. **Ascent:** 1969 ft / 600 metres
Estimated Time: 3-6 hours

Route: Cross the stile on the southern bank of the Nant-y-moch and take a path through thick grass towards the grassy, northern ridge of Y Garn. Follow the ridge all the way to the summit where there is an ancient cairn. From there turn east, following a fence which takes you

Looking towards Nant-y-moch reservoir from the summit of Pumlumon Fawr

past a plantation of trees. Where this plantation comes to an end, the fence turns north and will lead you all the way to the summit of Pumlumon Fawr. However, rather than remain close to the fence, a slight detour left away from it will give much better views in places. From the sumit of Pumlumon Fawr, where there is a cairn and a triangulation point, turn east-north-east, over the summit fence, and go down to the col before climbing the grassy slopes of Pen Pumlumon Llygad-bychan (which is not named on the 1:50 000 map). A small cairn marks the highest point and a boundary stone nearby has on it the letters WWW and a date. From here, walk north-east over easy ground for about a quarter of a mile (0.4 kilometres) to the corner of the fence where there is another boundary stone. You will need to return to this point later in the walk. In the meantime, however, descend east and then climb to the summit of Pen Pumlumon Arwystli. From there, return to the point mentioned earlier, and follow the fence along the ridge towards Pen Cerrig Tewion in the north-west. Before you reach Pen Cerrig Tewion choose a convenient place to descend west to the dam at Llyn Llygad Rheidol. Once across the dam, a track takes you back to the road beside Nant-y-moch reservoir where you turn left to return to the starting point.

12. The Black Mountains

THE BLACK MOUNTAINS in Gwent is an area of high and comparatively flat moorland and the peaks are, in fact, little more than points on the moorland where there is a slight rise in the ground. Once up from the valley, you can wander for miles with little difficulty or effort from one summit to the next. It is perhaps only Pen Cerrig Calch with its rocky summit which creates the sensation of being on a real mountain, but having said that the Black Mountains offers the adventurous walker an opportunity to roam for hours at a leisurely pace in an area of great beauty and usually in comparative peace. Both routes described here are lengthy but can be made into shorter walks.

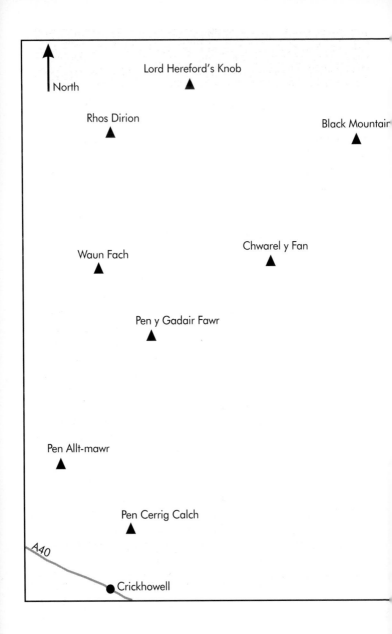

North

Lord Hereford's Knob ▲

Rhos Dirion ▲

Black Mountain ▲

Waun Fach ▲

Chwarel y Fan ▲

Pen y Gadair Fawr ▲

Pen Allt-mawr ▲

Pen Cerrig Calch ▲

A40

● Crickhowell

Mountain: Pen Cerrig Calch, 2300 ft / 701 m (72); Pen Allt-mawr, 2359 ft / 719 m (66); Waun Fach, 2657 ft / 810 m (32); Pen y Gadair Fawr, 2625 ft / 800 m (36)

Map: OS 161, OL 13: GR 217224, GR 207243, GR 215299, GR 229288

Translation: Limestone Head, Top of the Big Hillside, Little Moor, Top of the Great Seat

Pronunciation: Pen *Care*-rig Calch, Pen Allt-*ma*-oor, Wine Vaach, Pen uh *Gad*-ire *Va*-oor

Starting Point: Cwm Banw – a tight bend on a minor road three miles (4.8 kilometres) north of Crickhowell, GR 234229. Lay-by.

Distance: 14 miles / 22.4 kilometres. **Ascent:** 2850 ft / 869 metres

Estimated Time: 5-9 hours

Route: From the lay-by, cross the bridge and take the path on the southern side of the stream. Climb through the field to the lane above. Cross the lane and go up the lower slopes of Pen Cerrig Calch beside the wood. When you reach the top of the wood continue uphill in the same direction. The path soon bends rights and climbs steadily uphill. When the path levels out, by a substantial tree where the upper slopes of the mountain come into view, leave it and climb steeply south-west through heather, bracken and rocks directly to the rocky summit of Pen Cerrig Calch where there is a triangulation point. The hard work is now behind you. Follow the ridge – north-west at first – for a mile and a half (2.4 kilometres) to reach the triangulation point on the summit of Pen Allt-mawr. From there, a clear path heads north, turns to climb below the summit of Pen Twyn Glas and then turns north once more towards Mynydd Llysiau. (From the summit of Pen Twyn Glas a path follows the ridge of Tal Trwynau to the south-east and back to the car park, should you wish to curtail your walk.) The path north crosses the summit of Mynydd Llysiau and then descends to a col which is crossed by a second path. (This second path descends to the valley of the Grwyne Fechan to the east and offers another means of returning to the car park.) Having climbed steep slopes to Pen Trumau the path turns north-east to the summit of Waun Fach. From here, turn south-east and cross wet ground to reach Pen y Gadair Fawr. The path now becomes clearer once more as you follow the forest and continue across Pen Twyn Mawr. From Pen Twyn Mawr follow the forest south-east for about three quarters of a mile (1.2 kilometres) until you reach a cairn above Pen Gwyllt Meirch (GR 247255). Turn right (south-west) and descend heathery slopes to reach a good path which leads to a forest track (GR 243246). Cross the track and follow a wall to your left through the trees to the fields below. When you reach the forest once more (GR 238239), turn left along the path which follows the edge of the forest for about 300 yards (a quarter of a kilometre), then turn right and go down and across the river to the road. Cross over to the upper road and turn left to return to the car park.

Black Mountain

Mountain: Lord Hereford's Knob, 2231 ft / 680 m (87); Rhos Dirion, 2339 ft / 713 m (68); Chwarel y Fan, 2198 ft / 670 m (95); Black Mountain, 2297 ft / 700 m (73)

Map: OS 161, OL 13: GR 225350, GR 211334, GR 259293, GR 255354

Translation: Lord Hereford's Knob, Gentle Heath, Beacon Quarry, Black Mountain

Pronunciation: Lord Hereford's Knob, Rhowss *Dirry*-on, *Chwar*-rel uh Van, Black Mountain

Starting Point: Gospel Pass – the pass between Lord Hereford's Knob and Hay Bluff, about 5 miles south of Hay-on-Wye, GR 237350. Car park.

Distance: 14 miles / 22.4 kilometres. **Ascent:** 2400 ft / 732 metres

Estimated Time: 5-8 hours

Route: From the pass above the car park, a clear path climbs south-west and on to the summit of Lord Hereford's Knob. It is an easy walk from here to the triangulation point on Rhos Dirion a little over a mile away (about 1.8 kilometres) to the south-west. Now turn south-east and follow the long ridge above Grwyne Fawr reservoir for nearly four miles (about 6 kilometres) to the top of Chwarel y Fan. About three-quarters of a mile (1.2 kilometres) before you reach this summit, at a point where the ridge narrows and you start to climb towards a prominent, pointed outcrop, you pass a large cairn rather like a beehive (GR 251302). From the summit of Chwarel y Fan, return to this cairn. Turn right along a narrow path which soon trends north to skirt a cliff and then descends across the steep face of the hillside before reaching level ground, crossing a river and emerging at the Grange Trekking Centre. Once on the lane, turn right towards the hamlet of Capel-y-ffin. Turn left at the next junction and cross a bridge. (From here, you could walk along the road and back to the car park at the starting point.) The route now continues along the lane on the right by the church and across the Afon Honddu. Pass through a farmyard and continue south-east across fields towards the farm of Ty'r-onen and take the path just beyond which climbs steep slopes north to join Offa's Dyke Path on the ridge above. Turn left along Offa's Dyke Path – which here follows the border between England and Wales – for two miles (3.2 kilometres) to cross the unmarked summit of the Black Mountain (whose name is not marked on either map). Stay on the ridge to reach the triangulation point on Hay Bluff. From here, a path follows the edge of Ffynnon y Parc back to the car park.

13. Brecon Beacons

THIS IS THE MOST IMPRESSIVE and most popular group of mountains in South Wales. The group also includes the highest mountains in the South. These are splendid mountains which give generally easy, pleasant walking. The terrain is gentle, the paths are clear and the views — especially northwards — are extensive and splendid. The main peaks in the group — including Pen y Fan and Corn Du — are close to the main road from Brecon to Merthyr Tydfil and can be reached easily from the pass. However, this is not the best way to see or to approach these mountains and a different route is suggested here. To the west and east of the main peaks are others whose terrain is similar but which attract fewer walkers.

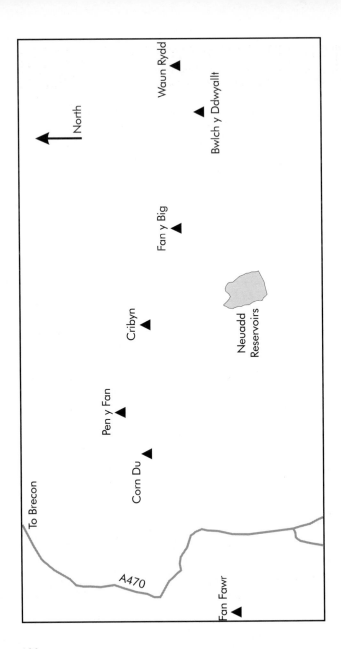

To Brecon

A470

North

Corn Du

Pen y Fan

Cribyn

Fan y Big

Bwlch y Ddwyallt

Waun Rydd

Neuadd Reservoirs

Fan Fawr

Mountain: Fan y Big, 2359 ft / 719 m (67); Cribyn, 2608 ft / 795 m (37), Pen y Fan, 2907 ft / 886 m (19); Corn Du, 2864 ft / 873 m (21)

Map: OS 160, OL 12: GR 036206, GR 023213, GR 012216, GR 007213

Translation: The Beak, Crest, Top of the Beacon, Black Horn

Pronunciation: Van uh *Beeg*, *Creeb*-in, Pen uh *Van*, Corn Dee

Starting Point: Taf Fechan Forest – the car park just south of Neuadd Reservoirs, GR 036171.

Distance: 8 ½ miles / 13.6 kilometres. **Ascent:** 2550 ft / 777 metres

Estimated Time: 4-6 hours

Route: From the car park, set off along the tarmac road towards the reservoirs. Leave it to take an ancient track which follows the edge of the forest and climbs steadily northwards towards the pass below Fan y Big. Opposite the northern end of the upper reservoir, turn north-east up the steep slopes to reach the ridge. Follow the ridge north to the flat summit of Fan y Big. Head down to the pass below Cribyn in the west and having crossed the ancient track climb the ridge of Craig Cwm Cynwyn to reach the stony summit of Cribyn. Once more, go down west to a col and climb another ridge – that of Craig Cwm Sere – to the triangulation point on the summit of Pen y Fan. The wide path to Corn Du in the south-west testifies to the popularity of the highest peaks in south Wales. Having crossed the gap of Bwlch Duwynt, however, you will probably see fewer people as you walk two miles (3.2 kilometres) south-east along the ridge to Graig Fan Ddu to pick up a path above the lower reservoir (GR 019183) which takes you down from the ridge, across open ground to cross the dam, and back to the tarmac road which leads to the car park.

Mountain: Fan Fawr, 2408 ft / 734 m (60)

Map: OS 160, OL 12: GR 970193
Translation: Large Beacon
Pronunciation: Van *Va*-oor
Starting Point: Car park opposite Storey Arms Outdoor Education Centre on the A470 between Brecon and Merthyr Tydfil, GR 983203.
Distance: 2 miles / 3.2 kilometres. **Ascent:** 968 ft / 295 metres
Estimated Time: 1-3 hours

Route: From the car park, the summit ridge of Fan Fawr can be seen above an intervening plateau. Cross one of the stiles and head south-west over easy slopes in the direction of the summit. Once on the plateau, the prominent north-east ridge comes into view, as do the cliff rocks high on the northern face of the mountain. Make straight for the north-east ridge. The ground becomes steeper as you gain height and the ridge narrows as it passes between the cliff on the north face and the hidden cliffs on the mountain's long east face. The path skirts these cliffs to reach the summit, marked by a few stones, which is on the cliff edge. A large triangulation point is to be seen lower down, to the south-west. It is well worth visiting, both for the views and for the feeling of isolation.

Mountain: Waun Rydd, 2523 ft / 769 m (46); Bwlch y Ddwyallt, 2474 ft / 754 m (51)

Map: OS 160 and 161, OL 12: GR 062206, GR 055203
Translation: Free Moorland, The Pass of the two Slopes
Pronunciation: Wine Reathe, Boolch uh *Thoo*-ee-allt
Starting Point: Tal-y-bont Reservoir. Car park on western side at GR 100197.
Distance: 7 miles / 11.2 kilometres. **Ascent:** 2031 ft / 619 metres
Estimated Time: 4-6 hours

Route: From the car park, walk north along the road for a hundred metres. After crossing the river bridge, turn left through a gate along a bridleway which, almost immediately, bears right to run parallell with the road. Follow signposts across fields and past two houses to reach a path by a stream. This path heads west, past trees and up steep slopes, towards the ridge of Twyn Du. Take this path all the way along the ridge climbing gradually to the steep slopes below the summit of Waun Rydd. The ground levels out above Craig Pwllfa and you now turn more to the north-west to reach the highest point, which is shown by the 769 height spot on the map and which is marked by a cairn. From here, drop west-south-west to the col below Bwlch y Ddwyallt. A path takes you south-south-west to the summit of Bwlch y Ddwyallt. Return to the col below Waun Rydd whose summit you do not need to re-visit as the main path skirts around east and back to the route of ascent.

14. Carmarthen Fan

THIS IS THE WESTERNMOST GROUP of mountains in south Wales. The most obvious feature of the main mountains in this group is the way they fall away suddenly towards Llyn y Fan Fawr and Llyn y Fan Fach. Like the other groups of mountains in south Wales, they have grassy summits and offer easy walking, and as in the Brecon Beacons one gets the feeling of standing high above the world as one looks down on the hilly, agricultural land below. Northwards, there are no other mountains to be seen — the nearest being the Pumlumon group, over 30 miles away.

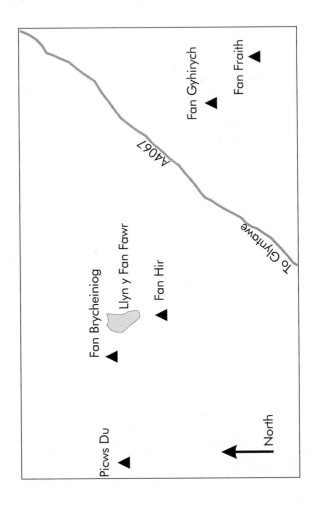

Fan Fraith

Fan Gyhirych

A4067

To Glyntawe

Fan Brycheiniog

Llyn y Fan Fawr

Fan Hir

Picws Du

North

Map: OS 160, OL 12: GR 831209, GR 825218, GR 812219

Translation: Long Beacon, Breconshire Beacon, Black Peak

Pronunciation: Van Heer, Van Brich-*aine*-eeog, *Pick*-oos Dee

Starting Point: The pass of Bwlch Cerrig Duon – on a minor road, 3 miles north of the A4067 near Glyntawe, GR 856223. There is room to park just off the road on the pass.

Distance: 9 miles / 14.4 kilometres. **Ascent:** 2034 ft / 620 metres

Estimated Time: 4-6 hours

Route: From the pass, a path crosses the lower slopes of Moel Feity towards Llyn y Fan Fawr, which lies on higher ground to the south-west and cannot be seen on approach. The path crosses rough ground above the southern end of the llyn and then climbs steeply up the edge to Bwlch Giedd. Once on the ridge, turn left and climb to the summit of Fan Hir. Return to the col and climb Fan Brycheiniog where there are two separate summits of equal height. The first is marked by a triangulation point and the second – which is about a quarter of a mile away (0.4 kilometres) – by a cairn. Picws Du can be seen about a mile away (1.6 kilometres) to the west and is reached by descending grassy slopes to the col (Bwlch Blaen-Twrch) and climbing its steep grassy slopes.

Picws Du

115

Mountain: Fan Gyhirych, 2379 ft / 725 m (64); Fan Fraith, 2192 ft / 668m (98)

Map: OS 160, OL 12: GR 880190, GR 887183

Translation: Beacon of the Gyhirych Stream, Speckled Beacon

Pronunciation: Van Guh-*heer*-ich, Van Vryeth

Starting Point: About two miles (3.2 kilometres) north of Glyntawe on the A4067. At the top of the pass, there is a lay-by on the right (east) side of the road shortly before you reach a tower on the left, GR 870194. **This path is closed during the lambing period between 15 April - 10 May.**

Distance: 3 miles / 4.8 kilometres. **Ascent:** 1360 ft / 415 metres

Estimated Time: 2-4 hours

Route: From the southern end of the car park a permissive path takes you directly onto the grassy and steep western slopes of Fan Gyhirych. The steepest section is just before the summit where there is a triangulation point. The summit is rough moorland with a ridge which extends eastwards. From the triangulation point on the summit, descend south-east to the road which separates Fan Gyhirych from Fan Fraith. Cross the road and head directly across wet ground to make the short climb to the summit of Fan Fraith. A few stones mark the highest point. Return by the same route or south-west (left) along the road.

The Welsh One Hundred

The Welsh 100 in Alphabetical Order

Name	No.	Height	Group	Page
Allt Fawr	75	2290/698	Blaenau Ffestiniog	62
Aran Benllyn	20	2904/885	Aran	81
Aran Fawddwy	16	2969/905	Aran	82
Arenig Fach	80	2260/689	Arenig	67
Arenig Fawr	24	2802/854	Arenig	68
Bera Bach	33	2648/807	Carneddau	18
Bera Mawr	38	2605/794	Carneddau	18
Black Mountain	73	2297/700	Black Mountains	105
Bwlch y Ddwyallt	51	2474/754	Brecon Beacons	111
Cadair Berwyn	28	2723/830	Berwyn	75
Cadair Bronwen	41	2575/785	Berwyn	75
Carnedd Dafydd	4	3412/1044	Carneddau	22
Carnedd Llewelyn	3	3491/1064	Carneddau	20
Carnedd y Ddelw	82	2257/688	Carneddau	19
Carnedd y Filiast (Arenig)	97	2195/669	Arenig	71
Carnedd y Filiast (Glyderau)	30	2697/822	Glyderau	33
Chwarel y Fan	95	2198/670	Black Mountains	105
Cnicht	79	2260/689	Blaenau Ffestiniog	59

Corn Du	21	2864/873	Brecon Beacons	109
Craig Cwm Amarch	39	2595/791	Cadair Idris	93
Craig Cwm Silyn	59	2408/734	Nantlle	51, 53
Creigiau Gleision	89	2224/678	Carneddau	26
Crib Goch	13	3028/923	Snowdon	40
Cribyn	37	2608/795	Brecon Beacons	109
Cyrniau Nod	100	2188/667	Berwyn	77
Diffwys	54	2461/750	Rhinog	90
Drosgl	49	2487/758	Carneddau	18
Drum	45	2526/770	Carneddau	19
Elidir Fawr	14	3018/920	Glyderau	33
Esgeiriau Gwynion	94	2201/671	Aran	83
Fan Brycheiniog	35	2631/802	Carmarthen Fan	115
Fan Fawr	60	2408/734	Brecon Beacons	110
Fan Fraith	98	2192/668	Carmarthen Fan	116
Fan Gyhirych	64	2379/725	Carmarthen Fan	116
Fan Hir	48	2497/761	Carmarthen Fan	115
Fan y Big	67	2359/719	Brecon Beacons	109
Foel Fras	11	3091/942	Carneddau	19
Foel Goch(by Elidir Fawr)	27	2726/831	Glyderau	33
Foel Grach	8	3202/976	Carneddau	19
Foel Hafod-fynydd	81	2260/689	Aran	83
Foel Wen	77	2267/691	Berwyn	75

Gallt yr Ogof	47	2503/763	Glyderau	35
Garnedd Goch	74	2297/700	Nantlle	51, 53
Garnedd Uchaf	12	3038/926	Carneddau	19
Garnedd Ugain	2	3494/1065	Snowdon	43
Glasgwm	43	2559/780	Aran	84
Glyder Fach	6	3261/994	Glyderau	30
Glyder Fawr	5	3278/999	Glyderau	31
Godor	88	2228/679	Berwyn	75
Gwaun y Llwyni	83	2247/685	Aran	82
Llwytmor	25	2785/849	Carneddau	17
Lord Hereford's Knob	87	2231/680	Black Mountains	105
Maesglase	92	2211/674	Cadair Idris	95
Moel Cynghorion	91	2211/674	Snowdon	47
Moel Druman	90	2218/676	Blaenau Ffestiniog	62
Moel Eilio	63	2382/726	Snowdon	47
Moel Hebog	42	2569/783	Nantlle	54
Moel Llyfnant	53	2464/751	Arenig	69
Moel Siabod	22	2861/872	Blaenau Ffestiniog	61
Moel Sych	29	2713/827	Berwyn	75
Moelwyn Bach	70	2329/710	Blaenau Ffestiniog	60
Moelwyn Mawr	44	2526/770	Blaenau Ffestiniog	60
Mynydd Drws-y-coed	76	2280/695	Nantlle	51
Mynydd Mawr	78	2264/690	Nantlle	55

Mynydd Moel	23	2831/863	Cadair Idris	93
Mynydd Perfedd	31	2667/813	Glyderau	33
Mynydd Tarw	86	2234/681	Berwyn	75
Pen Allt-mawr	66	2359/719	Black Mountains	103
Pen Cerrig Calch	72	2300/701	Black Mountains	103
Pen Llithrig y Wrach	40	2592/790	Carneddau	24
Pen Pumlumon Arwystli	58	2431/741	Pumlumon	99
Pen Pumlumon Llygad-bychan	62	2385/727	Pumlumon	99
Pen y Bryn Fforchog	84	2247/685	Aran	84
Pen y Fan	19	2907/886	Brecon Beacons	109
Pen y Gadair	18	2930/893	Cadair Idris	93
Pen y Gadair Fawr	36	2625/800	Black Mountains	103
Pen yr Helgi Du	26	2733/833	Carneddau	24
Pen yr Ole Wen	7	3209/978	Carneddau	23
Picws Du	55	2457/749	Carmarthen Fan	115
Pumlumon Fawr	52	2467/752	Pumlumon	99
Rhinog Fach	69	2336/712	Rhinog	89
Rhinog Fawr	65	2362/720	Rhinog	89
Rhobell Fawr	61	2408/734	Arenig	70
Rhos Dirion	68	2339/713	Black Mountains	105
Snowdon (Yr Wyddfa)	1	3560/1085	Snowdon	39
Tarren y Gesail	99	2188/667	Cadair Idris	96
Tomle	57	2434/742	Berwyn	75

Trum y Ddysgl	71	2326/709	Nantlle	51
Tryfan	15	3002/915	Glyderau	29
Waun Fach	32	2657/810	Black Mountains	103
Waun Oer	96	2198/670	Cadair Idris	95
Waun Rydd	46	2523/769	Brecon Beacons	111
Y Foel Goch (by Tryfan)	34	2641/805	Glyderau	35
Y Garn (Glyderau)	10	3107/947	Glyderau	32
Y Garn (Pumlumon)	85	2244/684	Pumlumon	99
Y Llethr	50	2480/756	Rhinog	89
Y Lliwedd	17	2946/898	Snowdon	44
Yr Aran	56	2451/747	Snowdon	46
Yr Elen	9	3156/962	Carneddau	21
Ysgafell Wen	93	2205/672	Blaenau Ffestiniog	62

The Welsh 100 by Height

No.	Name	Height	Group	Page
1	Snowdon (Yr Wyddfa)	3560/1085	Snowdon	39
2	Garnedd Ugain	3494/1065	Snowdon	43
3	Carnedd Llewelyn	3491/1064	Carneddau	20
4	Carnedd Dafydd	3412/1044	Carneddau	22
5	Glyder Fawr	3278/999	Glyderau	31
6	Glyder Fach	3261/994	Glyderau	30
7	Pen yr Ole Wen	3209/978	Carneddau	23
8	Foel Grach	3202/976	Carneddau	19
9	Yr Elen	3156/962	Carneddau	21
10	Y Garn (Glyderau)	3107/947	Glyderau	32
11	Foel Fras	3091/942	Carneddau	19
12	Garnedd Uchaf	3038/926	Carneddau	19
13	Crib Goch	3028/923	Snowdon	40
14	Elidir Fawr	3018/920	Glyderau	33
15	Tryfan	3002/915	Glyderau	29
16	Aran Fawddwy	2969/905	Aran	82
17	Y Lliwedd	2946/898	Snowdon	44
18	Pen y Gadair	2930/893	Cadair Idris	93

19	Pen y Fan	2907/886	Brecon Beacons	109
20	Aran Benllyn	2904/885	Aran	81
21	Corn Du	2864/873	Brecon Beacons	109
22	Moel Siabod	2861/872	Blaenau Ffestiniog	61
23	Mynydd Moel	2831/863	Cadair Idris	93
24	Arenig Fawr	2802/854	Arenig	68
25	Llwytmor	2785/849	Carneddau	17
26	Pen yr Helgi Du	2733/833	Carneddau	24
27	Foel Goch(by Elidir Fawr)	2726/831	Glyderau	33
28	Cadair Berwyn	2723/830	Berwyn	75
29	Moel Sych	2713/827	Berwyn	75
30	Carnedd y Filiast (Glyderau)	2697/822	Glyderau	33
31	Mynydd Perfedd	2667/813	Glyderau	33
32	Waun Fach	2657/810	Black Mountains	103
33	Bera Bach	2648/807	Carneddau	18
34	Y Foel Goch (by Tryfan)	2641/805	Glyderau	35
35	Fan Brycheiniog	2631/802	Carmarthen Fan	115
36	Pen y Gadair Fawr	2625/800	Black Mountains	103
37	Cribyn	2608/795	Brecon Beacons	109
38	Bera Mawr	2605/794	Carneddau	18
39	Craig Cwm Amarch	2595/791	Cadair Idris	93
40	Pen Llithrig y Wrach	2592/790	Carneddau	24

41	Cadair Bronwen	2575/785	Berwyn	75
42	Moel Hebog	2569/783	Nantlle	54
43	Glasgwm	2559/780	Aran	84
44	Moelwyn Mawr	2526/770	Blaenau Ffestiniog	60
45	Drum	2526/770	Carneddau	19
46	Waun Rydd	2523/769	Brecon Beacons	111
47	Gallt yr Ogof	2503/763	Glyderau	35
48	Fan Hir	2497/761	Carmarthen Fan	115
49	Drosgl	2487/758	Carneddau	18
50	Y Llethr	2480/756	Rhinog	89
51	Bwlch y Ddwyallt	2474/754	Brecon Beacons	111
52	Pumlumon Fawr	2467/752	Pumlumon	99
53	Moel Llyfnant	2464/751	Arenig	69
54	Diffwys	2461/750	Rhinog	90
55	Picws Du	2457/749	Carmarthen Fan	115
56	Yr Aran	2451/747	Snowdon	46
57	Tomle	2434/742	Berwyn	75
58	Pen Pumlumon Arwystli	2431/741	Pumlumon	99
59	Craig Cwm Silyn	2408/734	Nantlle	51, 53
60	Fan Fawr	2408/734	Brecon Beacons	110
61	Rhobell Fawr	2408/734	Arenig	70
62	Pen Pumlumon Llygad-bychan	2385/727	Pumlumon	99

63	Moel Eilio	2382/726	Snowdon	47
64	Fan Gyhirych	2379/725	Carmarthen Fan	116
65	Rhinog Fawr	2362/720	Rhinog	89
66	Pen Allt-mawr	2359/719	Black Mountains	103
67	Fan y Big	2359/719	Brecon Beacons	109
68	Rhos Dirion	2339/713	Black Mountains	105
69	Rhinog Fach	2336/712	Rhinog	89
70	Moelwyn Bach	2329/710	Blaenau Ffestiniog	60
71	Trum y Ddysgl	2326/709	Nantlle	51
72	Pen Cerrig Calch	2300/701	Black Mountains	103
73	Black Mountain	2297/700	Black Mountains	105
74	Garnedd Goch	2297/700	Nantlle	51, 53
75	Allt Fawr	2290/698	Blaenau Ffestiniog	62
76	Mynydd Drws-y-coed	2280/695	Nantlle	51
77	Foel Wen	2267/691	Berwyn	75
78	Mynydd Mawr	2264/690	Nantlle	55
79	Cnicht	2260/689	Blaenau Ffestiniog	59
80	Arenig Fach	2260/689	Arenig	67
81	Foel Hafod-fynydd	2260/689	Aran	83
82	Carnedd y Ddelw	2257/688	Carneddau	19
83	Gwaun y Llwyni	2247/685	Aran	82
84	Pen y Bryn Fforchog	2247/685	Aran	84

85	Y Garn (Pumlumon)	2244/684	Pumlumon	99
86	Mynydd Tarw	2234/681	Berwyn	75
87	Lord Hereford's Knob	2231/680	Black Mountains	105
88	Godor	2228/679	Berwyn	75
89	Creigiau Gleision	2224/678	Carneddau	26
90	Moel Druman	2218/676	Blaenau Ffestiniog	62
91	Moel Cynghorion	2211/674	Snowdon	47
92	Maesglase	2211/674	Cadair Idris	95
93	Ysgafell Wen	2205/672	Blaenau Ffestiniog	62
94	Esgeiriau Gwynion	2201/671	Aran	83
95	Chwarel y Fan	2198/670	Black Mountains	105
96	Waun Oer	2198/670	Cadair Idris	95
97	Carnedd y Filiast (Arenig)	2195/669	Arenig	71
98	Fan Fraith	2192/668	Carmarthen Fan	116
99	Tarren y Gesail	2188/667	Cadair Idris	96
100	Cyrniau Nod	2188/667	Berwyn	77

The Welsh One Hundred Club

Anyone who walks to the summits of all the mountains listed in this book is invited to contact me via the publisher to join the **Welsh One Hundred Club**. A special form will be sent to you to register your achievement and then a certificate will be issued. A list will be kept of all those who register and a Welsh One Hundred Club newsletter will be circulated. You can also visit my website for updates and features on mountaineering in Wales – **http://www.ylolfa.com/welsh100**

I would also welcome any comments on the routes described here and indeed on any aspect of this book or of walking the mountains of Wales. I would particularly like to know about any difficulties encountered by walkers on these mountains.

Dafydd Andrews, c/o Y Lolfa, Talybont, Ceredigion, SY24 5AP, Wales; e-*mail:* welsh100@ylolfa.com